H02B

CW01499080

The Hidden Power
of Vibrations

The Hidden Power of Vibrations

HARVEY DAY

PELHAM BOOKS   LONDON

First published in Great Britain by
Pelham Books Ltd
52 Bedford Square
London WC1B 3EF
1979

ISBN 0 7207 1134 7

Printed in Great Britain by
REDWOOD BURN LIMITED
Trowbridge & Esher

Contents

I
The Nature
of Vibrations

'So the people shouted when the priests blew with the trumpets; and it came to pass, when the people heard the sound of the trumpets, and the people shouted with a great shout, that the wall fell down flat, so that the people went up into the city, every man straight before him, and they took the city.' (Joshua 6. 20.)

Every child knows the story of the fall of Jericho but few except fundamentalists believe it to be anything but a garbled version of the actual event. 'How on earth,' succeeding generations have asked, 'could the sound of trumpets have demolished stone walls?'

Today we are not so sure. Science has proved that there is more than a scintilla of substance in the story, and many of the Biblical stories have a rational foundation.

CARUSO SHATTERED A WINE GLASS

That vibrations can affect matter has been shown to be true time and again. At the turn of the nineteenth century, when Dr Albert Abrams was travelling in Italy, he stayed in Naples, where he saw Caruso, the famous tenor, flick a wine glass with a finger to produce a pure tone. Then he put down the glass, stepped back a few paces and reproduced the same note, shattering the glass to fragments and proving that matter can be affected when the appropriate vibrations have been produced.

When Dublin Airport first went into commission the screech of the jets coming in produced, in those surroundings, peculiar vibrations which shattered the glasses in the bar, and this happened with such regularity that eventually plastic tumblers were substituted.

A THICK TUMBLER EXPLODED BY SOUND

There have been numerous such incidents, not all of which have been recorded. A Mr T. McArthur of Lanarkshire, for instance, wrote to a newspaper in 1974, saying: 'I was watching BBC 1 last night when a female soloist hit a particularly high note while singing "Praise The Lord". The results were spectacular, for a thick empty glass tumbler on a shelf next to my head exploded. It cracked down one side, was completely severed three-quarters of the way down and the half-inch base parted into three portions.'

OPAL DESTROYED BY A SINGLE NOTE

Diamonds are among the hardest substances known and experts say that if a diamond is dropped from four or five feet on to concrete it is liable to shatter. The same is true of most gems, which contain fissures so fine that they cannot be seen even under a powerful magnifying glass, and fluoroscopes are used to detect these cracks when they have to be cut. An involuntary demonstration of the flaws in opals occurred in 1966 during a farewell dinner to Group Captain R. C. Haine at Lindholme near Doncaster.

An RAF band was in attendance and Chief Technician Tichmarsh hit the high note E above C, at which an opal ring worth £50, worn by one of the guests, disintegrated!

In each of these instances the destruction of the walls of Jericho was produced on a miniature scale.

THE THEORY OF VIBRATIONS

The theory of vibrations is not new. The yogis tell us that the constant repetition of appropriate mantras (sounds, syllables or phrases with sacred or spiritual associations) can increase sensitivity and spiritual awareness. In India, Ceylon and Burma there are men known as mantra-karas who will compose a mantra to achieve a specific purpose, such as a cure for disease or the increase of intuition, extrasensory perception or other psychic powers. The most powerful of all mantras is the magical 'OM', which pronounced in the right way will set up health-giving vibrations in the head, chest and right down to the solar plexus, the seat of power and of the emotions.

One such practitioner is Cyrus D. F. Abayakoon, son of one of the chiefs through whom Britain ruled Ceylon in the days of the raj, who now lives in London. In his youth he studied astrology under the guidance of Buddhist priests, mastered the *nadi-granthams* (the art of reading ready-made horoscopes inscribed on palm leaves – like papyri – centuries ago and handed down) and grew interested in mantra-yoga, which is based on the belief that all matter consists of vibrations that can heal or destroy, cause joy or sorrow, or change one's mental outlook and mentality. In Ceylon there are Buddhists who cure the bites of poisonous reptiles by repeating mantras, so he reasoned: 'If mantras can cure snakebites, why not other adverse conditions?' He made an extensive study of the subject and has since cured many people of deep-seated illnesses which have baffled orthodox physicians.

DURAISWAMI IYER

Another practitioner of mantras was Duraiswami Iyer, known

throughout India as 'the Poison King' because he could cure snakebite, epileptic fits and other diseases at a distance by means of mantras.* A newspaper article described that all one had to do was to send a telegram to Elamanur, South India, where he lived. On receiving it he would tear a strip from his dhoti (a voluminous nether garment), repeat a mantra to fit the condition and the victim would be cured. Snakebites were cured free but other sufferers were charged. According to reliable witnesses he had thousands of cures to his credit.

SHRI NARSIAH

The late Kenneth Anderson, author of a number of books on jungle life in India, who talks about mantras and their power, relates that while he was in the telegraph department of the Southern Railway there was stationed at Polreddipalayam in the state of Andra Pradesh a humble postmaster named Shri Narsiah, who was instrumental in saving the lives of hundreds of snakebite victims, the author among them.†

The people in that region were extremely poor, but if one was bitten all he or his relatives and friends had to do was to hurry to the nearest post office, give the name and address of the victim and say 'Snakebite'. It was an unwritten rule that such messages received priority over all others and were sent free.

The moment Shri Narsiah received such a telegram he would go to a sacred tree outside the station, tear a strip from his dhoti, tie it to a branch and repeat the sacred mantra in a semi-audible tone. Provided the snake had not already been killed, it would die and the victim would be cured!

Anderson, who had no fear of snakes and handled them with impunity, was once careless while handling a cobra,

* *Manchester Evening News*: 25 July 1951.

† Kenneth Anderson, *Jungles Long Ago* (George Allen and Unwin, 1976).

which freed its head for an instant and sank its fangs into his arm. He threw it into a box, slapped down the lid and raced in his car to the nearest hospital. There he was told that their stock of antitoxin had run out. Soon the venom started to take effect and he began to feel giddy. Those in his home had little faith in hospitals, however, so one of them dashed 400 yards to the telegraph office and a 'snakebite' wire was soon in Narsiah's hands. He intoned the magic mantra and, though hundreds of miles away, Anderson felt better. When he looked into the box where he had thrown the cobra, it was dead.

MAGIC MUSIC

Equally inexplicable to the layman is the source of music which is heard in the ancient temple in Perayoor, six miles from Pudukottai, in the month of Masi each year. According to T. R. Vythinatha Aiyar, former member of the Legislative Council: 'Inside the temple there is a tilt (*sunai* in Tamil) which is always full of water. When the water reaches a certain level in the tilt we suddenly hear heavenly music coming from underneath the water. We hear *nathaswaram*, the chanting of mantras, the playing of violins, *mridangam*, veena, dance bells, conch, etc. It lasts for nearly two hours. The pious used to take a bath, chant mantras on the sides of the tilt and wait for the music. A former raja had a road built from Pudukottai to Perayoor so that he might visit the temple without delay.'*

VIBRATIONS AND RELIGION

Instinctively the founders of all great religions have made intelligent use of the repetitions of chanted prayers and litanies and the vibrations they radiate, and it is not without reason that the organ is the main instrument for accompanying sing-

* *The Hindu*, March 1950.

ing, chanting and all such ceremonies, for no other known instrument reverberates so magnificently and produces music of such awe and reverence. The minds of worshippers enveloped in such sound are transported from mundane matters into the world of the spiritual, where neither reason nor logic prevails.

We have long scoffed at the 'ignorant' Tibetan who whirls his prayer wheel as he repeats the magic formula: '*Om mani padme kam!*' ('Behold the jewel of the lotus flower!') but the litanies of the Christian Church are repetitions of supplications which originally were meant to be chanted aloud and earnestly, using the chest as a bellows and the head as a sounding board. When the Church was founded the masses were ignorant and the priests gave no reasons for ritual and intonation. Now we realize that the breathing involved was beneficial to health and the vibrations induced during singing and prayer induced feelings of peace and contentment, and were instrumental in dissipating neurotic conditions, which if allowed to develop would have produced the psychosomatic diseases from which so many millions suffer today.

CHURCH-GOING HABIT

Millions of people who are not deeply religious go to church from habit. On emerging they often say: 'I feel much better for going.' Of course they do. As they intoned the responses they breathed deeply. They sang and listened *in silence* with only their thoughts for company. This experience they shared with others, which is always more moving than in isolation, for the vibrations around us, both good and bad, affect us. That is why quite sensible people often behave outrageously when in crowds. We call it mob-psychology, for mobs are driven by enthusiasm, which is endemic, and often resort to violence under the influence of mass vibrations.

Slowly it has dawned on the West that vibrations are all-powerful. They are the substance of matter. Every object, living and inanimate, emits vibrations which radiate through space.

THE SHIVAPUR STONE

About 24 kilometres south of Poona, India, lies a village called Shivapur, known to the outside world only because it boasts a mosque dedicated to the Sufi saint Qumar Ali Dervish. On the lawn in front rests a granite boulder weighing approximately 125 lb.

When a group of pilgrims and perhaps a tourist or two have gathered outside, the bearded *maulvi* (priest) greets them and asks for eleven volunteers. He then explains that if eleven stand round the boulder, lean over and touch the stone with their index fingers and simultaneously chant '*Qumar Ali Dervish!*' in ringing tones, the block will rise to a height of just over 6 feet. As soon as the chant dies away it falls with a thud, so pilgrims are warned to keep their feet out of the way.

The words must be chanted at a certain pitch and if more or fewer than eleven place their fingers on the stone, it will not rise. Why this is so no one can explain, but the demonstration takes place frequently – as many as six times a day and every day of the year.

There is also another boulder weighing about 100 lb which requires the same chant, though the index fingers of only nine are needed to raise it aloft.

THE BOULDER OF TAY NINU ANNAM

This is by no means the only unexplained miracle caused by the power of vibrations. In Cambodia there is a vast boulder weighing 300 tons known as Tay Ninu Annam which hangs permanently in mid-air without any visible means of support. The Cambodians believe that it is supported by the vibrations emitted by the chanting of priests, worshippers and pilgrims who constantly intone a certain mantra. This has been going on, as far as one can gather, for centuries.

VIBRATIONS HAVE WAVE FORMS

If a stone is dropped into a pool of water a number of concentric circles are formed, decreasing in size till they appear to die away. All vibrations take wave forms. Some seem to die fairly soon but that is because they lose their strength; others are projected millions of miles into space, bounce off objects such as planets or stars, and return to earth. The power of vibrations, the distances they cover and the ways in which they act often baffle us.

PIEZO-ELECTRIC EFFECT

The science of vibrations is a comparatively recent one. Till 1880 no one had any idea how they acted. Then the Curie brothers found that if an electric current was passed through a crystal, a substance which was thought to be a non-conductor, the size of the crystal was altered by an infinitesimal amount. They called this phenomenon the 'piezo-electric' effect, but then abandoned their experiments, which appeared to have little practical value.

Three years later Sir Francis Galton used piezo-electricity to produce an ultrasonic whistle which could be heard by dogs but not by humans. This was considered a freakish achievement but also seemed to have little practical value.

The information discovered by the Curies gathered dust in files for thirty-seven years, by which time Britain, France and their allies were at war with Germany and ships were being sunk in large numbers by U-boats in the Atlantic. Britain, which depended on food and raw materials from abroad, would soon have been starved into submission had scientists not clutched at the most bizarre ideas to counter the submarine menace.

PROFESSOR LANGEVIN

For years Professor Paul Langevin, famous for his researches into X-rays, magnetism and the theory of relativity, had been experimenting with electric currents. He pored over the Curies' discovery and came up with three ideas which he put into practice.

(1) He sent an electric current through a crystal thousands of times a second in order to transform it into a vibrating source of supersonic waves which could be transmitted through water. He used Direct Current (DC) but failed to achieve the results he expected.

(2) He then decided to use Alternating Current (AC) because there is an instant during reversal when no current is flowing, and though this period is infinitesimal, the crystal reverts to its normal length for a minute fraction of a second. If, therefore, the current changes a thousand times a second the crystal vibrates the same number of times, producing supersonic waves, and the frequency desired can be produced by the number of changes.

(3) In his third experiment a number of crystals were connected in such a way that a beam of concentrated supersound could be made to pierce water and detect any metal object in the depths of the sea. He was sure that it was possible to concentrate a sound beam in the way a lens concentrates a beam of light. The sound would strike a hidden submarine and bounce back to the crystal, making it vibrate again, and simple calculations based on the time it took for the echo to return gave the depth and position of the submarine, which could then be destroyed by depth charges.

Langevin's discovery was revolutionary, not only for war but for peaceful purposes. One of his contemporaries said: 'He revealed what the eye cannot see by using what the ear cannot hear,' and his invention did more than any other to save the Allies from defeat – yet, how many apart from scientists have heard of Langevin?

WHAT IS SOUND?

Sound consists of vibrations which travel in waves. When you talk, sing, shout, clap your hands, drop an object or make vigorous motions, vibrations are produced. The vibrations or ripples generated by speech travel comparatively slowly: at about 1100 feet a second and may be produced at anything from 30 to 20,000 a second. These we call cycles. Human eardrums fail to register them if they are either below or above these limits. A bass note registers at about 20–30 cycles a second. If it rises to 10,000 the sound will change to treble. There is also a borderline beyond which some people with extra-keen hearing can detect sound but those without cannot; for instance, the cry of a bat. Dogs can pick up super-sound to which we are oblivious and that is why they sometimes prick up their ears when we hear nothing. Most pet shops sell 'silent' whistles for dogs.

LEVELS OF SOUND

The following two pages may be skipped by most readers as they will interest only those with a technical background.

Infrasonics
These range from 0 to 16 cycles, 16 being the lower limit of audibility for humans.

Audible Range
From 16 to 20,000 cycles. The characteristic pitch of a man's voice is 125; that of a woman 250. A thousand cycles is known as the reference frequency of sound measurements.

Ultrasonics or Supersonics
From 16,000 to just over 20,000 cycles, produced by the rapid vibration of a quartz crystal making use of the piezo-electrical effect. The upper limit of insect sounds if 32,000 and the lower limit for most biological and chemical effects is 100,000. Most germs and other forms of bacteria are destroyed at

1,000,000 cycles, which is also the frequency used in marine signalling, surveying and submarine detection. About fifty years ago the upper limit of vibrations was 16,000,000 a second, but now scientists work in the realms of the fantastic, and Hertzian* waves range above 3×10^{10} cycles a second! That any activity can take place so many times a second seems beyond the power of imagination.

It is difficult to transmit high-frequency waves through air and even more so to pass ultrasonic waves through air into liquids or solids, and vice versa. Ultrasonic waves are therefore confined to liquids and solids and have frequencies measured in millions of cycles rather than thousands. Like sound, ultrasonic waves need a transmission medium of some sort, for unlike radio waves they cannot travel through a vacuum.

Decibel

It is commonly accepted that the measure of sound is the decibel, but that is not so. The correct unit of measurement is the phon. A sound has the intensity of 100 phons if it is 100 decibels lower than the softest sound of that pitch audible to the human ear. The decibel is expressed as dB or one tenth of a bel.

Bel

This is the logarithmic relationship of the difference between two noise or energy levels.

Hertz

Hertz (Hz) is the name, by international agreement, for the number of repetitions of similar pressure variations per second of time; a unit of frequency which previously was called 'cycles per second' (cps or C/s). The decibel is the common measure of sound pressure.

* Named after Heinrich Hertz (1857–94), a physicist noted for investigation into the relation between electricity and light, especially for his discoveries of electrical waves of large amplitude (Hertzian waves) in wireless telegraphy.

The Effect of Sound on the Human Ear

Sound does not exist without an apparatus with which to convert vibrations into sound, such as the human ear. The sound may be acceptable and even pleasant, such as music, or unbearable and unpleasant, such as an explosion. If trees fall on a desert island or waves smash themselves on a rock-bound coast vibrations are produced, but not sound, for there is no apparatus to convert them.

The dB Scale*

Sounds are measured on the dB scale and range from 200 dB, which is the typical sound of a noise weapon, down to the threshold of hearing. Some dB measurements are given below:

180   Lethal level.

150   Sound at speech frequencies which can burn the skin.

130   Jet engine at 100 feet; air siren; pneumatic riveter; hydraulic press at three feet.

120   Threshold of pain, a billion times greater than the least audible sound; jet aircraft at 500 feet; inside a boiler factory.

110   Motor horn at 20 feet; pop group at four feet; power mower at four feet; train whistle at 50 feet; hammer blows on steel.

100   Food blender at two feet; inside train compartment when door is slammed; lorry that passed MoT test of 92 decibels at 25 feet measured in a narrow street at 12 feet (furthest distance to which a pedestrian can retreat).

90   Heavy truck; automatic lathe; underground train.

80   Danger level; inside small car; noisy office; alarm clock; average heavy traffic.

70   Busy street; large shop; building noise.

60   Normal conversation at three feet.

50   Quiet street; inside average home.

40   Quiet office; quiet conversation.

* Facts supplied by the Noise Abatement Society.

30   Tick of watch; rustle of paper; whisper.
20   Quiet country lane.
10   Leaves rustling in the wind.
 0   Threshold of hearing.

WHAT IS MATTER

Just over a century ago it was believed that all matter was either solid, liquid or gaseous. Solids are objects that can be felt and though sometimes malleable will resist the pressure of fingers. The matter in a solid is coherent.

Liquids are states of matter in which the particles move freely over each other. They have a definite volume but assume the shape of any vessel into which they are poured; thus, a liquid is matter in a state between a solid and a gas.

Gases are substances which will always occupy the entire space of any containing vessel and consist of molecules moving freely in space. A molecule is the smallest portion of any substance existing independently and retaining the properties of the original substance.

GEORGE LAKHOVSKY

These definitions sufficed until in the Twenties George Lakhovsky, a Russian engineer, put forward the theory that the basis of life is not matter, but vibrations. He said that 'every living thing emits radiations, and cells, the essential organic units of all living bodies, emit and absorb high frequency waves.' This applies not only to human cells but to the cells of plants and possibly to the cells of what we term inanimate matter. If this is true then all matter is one, as the yogis have claimed for 6000 years, and is interchangeable. Which accounts for the fact that the molecules of such substances as iron, bismuth, calcium, phosphorus, magnesium, chlorine and what we call the 'trace elements' – manganese, lead, copper, etc – can affect the human system and cure disease, or kill, depending on the quantities ingested.

Humans have an affinity with the *whole of Nature*.

SMALLER THAN ATOMS

Fifty years ago children were taught that the atom was the smallest particle in Nature, and two atoms comprised one molecule. In 1964 Mr Murray Gell-Mann put forward the theory that there were particles smaller than atoms and in 1969 Professor Charles McCusker of Sydney University proved that there were, and he called them *quarks*. They are so minute that it takes three of them to make one of the protons or neutrons which form the nucleus of a single atom.

ONE-BILLIONTH OF A MILLIMETRE

Rash is the person who scoffs at any theory, no matter how improbable. Scarcely a year passes without the impossible being converted into reality. Not long ago Professor Werner Heisenberg of Goettingen, Germany, a Nobel Prize winner and one of the founders of nuclear physics, claimed to have discovered a new constant in nature – the shortest length – which he calculated as one billionth of a millimetre, and went on to explain that in this unimaginably tiny space occur all the interactions of particles within the nucleus of an atom.

We are apt to think that the discovery of atoms as the smallest known particles is a recent one, but the Hindu sage Aulukya propounded a similar theory 2800 years ago, which was fully explained in *Vaisesika*, one of the six systems of Indian philosophy. He called the smallest speck of matter *paramanu* and said that two *paramanus* comprised one *anu* or atom, and three *anus* a *trasarenu*.

CONCEPT OF TIME

The Ancient Hindus even divided time into unimaginable fractions. Their smallest measure of time was also called a *paramanu*, which was the time taken by sunlight to flit across the diameter of one *paramanu*. Two *paramanus* made one *anu*; three *anus* one *trasaranu*, and the time taken for light to traverse three *trasaranus* was known as a *truti*. A *vedha* consisting of 100 *trutis* was known as a *lava*, and three *lavas* made one *nimesa* or twinkling of an eye; and three *nimesas* made one *kshana* or moment. What use they made of these tiny measurements is not known, but they must have been used for some form of scientific experiment.

The Vedic seers managed in some mysterious way to determine the speed of light, its wave motions and composition, though how this was accomplished without the accurate instruments we now possess remains a mystery. We know, however, that their knowledge of astronomy in general, and that of the northern and southern constellations, was detailed and extensive.

Professor Benjamin Farringdon said in a talk on the Third Programme of the BBC that evidence exists that the Hindus knew about atomic energy, and Professor Soddy, the physicist, that one of their writings describes an explosion as having 'the brightness of a thousand suns'. Possibly misuse of their knowledge destroyed their civilization and records, as it may eventually destroy ours.

The ancient Chinese may also have invented an atomic bomb, for when tests were carried out recently in the Gobi Desert the intense heat produced a glass substance similar to the vitreous sand that has existed in the vicinity for thousands of years.

NOISE

Noise is one of the curses of the modern age.

There has never been a noisier age. Noise seems to increase as we progress and grow more civilized and harness more mechanical monsters to do our bidding. The pleasant noises of the past – barking dogs, lowing cattle, cackling hens, crowing roosters, iron tyres on cobbled roads and the musical clip-clop of hooves – have given place to the roar of 40-ton trucks, snorting diesel engines, the exhausts of sports cars and motorcycles, road drills, tube trains and jet planes.

THE HUMAN EAR

The human ear has a remarkable ability to accustom itself to sound in volume; sudden shattering noise is unnerving and sends the blood pressure rocketing. The young scamp who fills a paper bag with air and bursts it behind grandpa's chair when the old boy is having forty winks after lunch, making him leap three feet into the air as if injected with morphine or nitroglycerine (two of the most powerful drugs for increasing blood pressure within the brain) may be shortening his life appreciably, and the slamming of car doors after midnight has ruined many a light sleeper's rest.

Motorcycle exhausts can be even more shattering, and the authorities have a duty to insist on efficient silencers being fitted. Just after the Second World War the Velocette Company produced a 250 hp machine that purred almost noiselessly, and BSA a sloping-cylinder 500 hp motorcycle that was also very quiet. If two makers could make silent machines, why not others? In 1936 Mr F. Servais and his son Norman invented a silencer for internal combustion engines that should have taken the motoring world by storm. When fitted to a noisy motorcycle the only sound that could be heard was that of the tyres on the tarred road! Several buses were fitted with the device, and the City of Westminster adopted the silencer on their night sweepers. Why it did not become a standard fitting on all motorcycles and cars remains a mystery. Perhaps because the young revel in noise and like to impress their girl friends as they accelerate violently from a standing start.

A little consideration by the noisier elements in our society would make life much pleasanter for the rest of us, for research has shown that 90 per cent of the noise we suffer in crowds is made by 10 per cent of those in them.

The human ear acts as a bandpass filter. In simple terms the cochlea and its associate net nerves seem to act as a large set of overlapping bandpass filters connected in parallel. The outer and inner ear seem to be able to transmit pressure wave forms of sound to the inner ear to protect it from having to operate on sounds outside its capacity.

The middle ear prevents the transmission to the inner ear of pressure waves which have 'rise times' (maximum frequencies) in excess of 200 microseconds by means of the Eustachian* tube, and so save the eardrum from rupture.

When intensely high pressure hits the small muscles in the middle ear, they contract, stiffen the ossicular chain and damp down the sound. If the sound is very intense the ossicular chain appears to rotate on its normal axis in such a way that the pressure is limited or reduced. There are limits beyond which protection cannot go, however, such as bomb blasts or a heavy naval gun fired near a person who is not equipped with protective ear pads.

In America where cities and factories are much noisier than in Britain stringent laws are enforced to prevent excessive noise. The US Department of Labor specifies that employees of government contractors shall not be exposed for more than eight hours each day to noise at a steady level exceeding 90 dB (A), or acoustic decibels, and if such conditions are ignored any loss of hearing will entitle the sufferer to compensation.†

There are loopholes in this law, as in most, for the authorities appear to have ignored many noises of low frequency in the region of 2000 Hz when the standards were set.

---

* Named after Bartolomeo Eustachio, born in 1552, Professor of Anatomy at the Papal College in Rome; noted for his description of the thin tubes which connect ear and throat.

† Federal Register, Safety & Health Standards, US Dept of Labor, Washington DC, 1969. Effects of Airborne Ultrasound on Humans: Intl. Aud. 5.1966.

Excessive noise in factories and airfields is not merely terrifying; it undermines health. Jet engines, high-speed dental drills and so-called ultrasonic cleaners can cause intense discomfort, and long exposure to the noise they create results in tinnitus, dizziness, headaches, nausea and a feeling of 'fullness' in the ears. Sometimes the diseases they cause are psychosomatic (the result of fear of such noise) and experts say that any acoustic energy at high frequencies which affects humans does so through the inner ear.*

In America numerous law suits have been brought, many successfully, against airlines and their operators for creating 'intolerable noise', and papers and reports have been published by the US Government, including: L. M. Tondel, *Noise Litigation at Public Airports*; *A Report of the Jet Aircraft Noise Panel* (Office of Science and Technology, Executive Office of the President, 1966); and *Tests at Edwards Airforce Base, at Wallops Island, Virginia, and at Farnborough Airport*.

NOISE CAN DESTROY HEALTH

In a highly developed society such as ours, a certain amount of excessive noise is unavoidable and is the price we pay for progress. Among the worst are noises which stimulate sleepers, for they damage health even if the victim sleeps through, and is unaware of them.† Richter, a medical scientist who specializes in noise-induced illness, conducted a series of experiments during which he observed the EEG and VCR (vascoconstrictive) responses every thirty seconds to the sound of cars, trains and motorcycles passing the test room, even

---

* *Federal Register, Safety & Health Standards*: vol. 34, No. 12, part II (US Dept of Labor, 1969).

† R. Richter, *Sleep Disturbances Which We Are Not Aware Of, Caused by Traffic Noises* (US Government, 1966).

though the subjects slept soundly and had no recollection of such noises on wakening.

Graphs showed that the vegetative system is withdrawn from the recovery and strengthening processes during sleep, which are essential if the body is to be alkalinized. The body contains acids and alkalines, and in good health it is rather more alkaline than acid. If it becomes more acid than it should we fall ill, or even die. During sleep the alkalinizing process goes on, and that is why sound sleep, undisturbed by excessive noise, is essential to health – doubly so when a person is recovering from illness. A soothing sound such as a lullaby can aid recovery whereas the noise of passing cars and motorcycles will retard it. That is why hospitals and sanatoria should be situated on sites remote from noise.

WOMEN AND NOISE

Contrary to expectation, tests carried out in Britain and Sweden show that women, if not impervious to noise, endure it with greater equanimity than men. Mr D. L. Chadwick, consultant ear, nose and throat surgeon to the Manchester Royal Infirmary, told a group of delegates – mainly managers and engineers – that the effects of noise were modified by individual response, and possibly by sex, and women at a brewery bottling plant where noise levels were high were far less concerned and affected than men. 'They worked quite happily,' commented Mr Chadwick, 'and the noise did not bother them.' Similar tests carried out in Scandinavia supported this view.

Mr Chadwick advised that all who seek to enter an occupation where noise is well above the normal level should have a full and detailed assessment of their hearing before starting, and thereafter tests should be carried out at regular intervals to find out whether hearing has been affected. Only in this way can courts decide whether damages can be awarded in cases of industrial deafness.

NOISE WILL INCREASE

Unless silencers far more efficient than those already in use are invented, and some means found to muffle the noise in factories, the threshold of noise will double by 1980. This was the gloomy conclusion arrived at during the Conference on Noise in Transportation in Southampton in June 1974. The chairman, Professor Eifyn Richards of Loughborough University, said that the chief culprits were heavy diesel lorries, buses and to a lesser extent motorcycles. Though cars form the vast majority of vehicles on the roads they contribute comparatively little. He said that noise levels can be controlled and reduced but existing legislation had actually led to an *increase* of noise in heavy vehicles.

'Since we brought out the idea of noise limits for vehicles in the Wilson Report in 1963,' he said, 'there has been a substantial increase of seven decibels or so. Basically this is because manufacturers whose vehicles are not up to the limit have since been designing up to it. I would like to see a reduction of one decibel a year.'*

WAR ON NOISE IN RUSSIA

In the Soviet Union the health hazards of noise are fully appreciated and the government agrees that noise is one of the worst scourges in modern life. More than 12,000 specialists work in six research institutes belonging to the trade unions, fifteen institutes deal with hygienic and occupational diseases, and 219 departments of higher education establishments are collaborating to find ways to combat noise. The oldest noise laboratory in the country was set up in Leningrad about thirty-five years ago, and today Moscow has two scientific establishments devoted to the problem of getting rid of noise in light industry.

* *Guardian*: 21 July 1974.

Special measures have been introduced to reduce noise in industrial establishments, noisy jobs must not be undertaken in built-up areas at night, and all factories have been instructed to do their utmost to reduce noise. Stringent regulations have been enforced to ensure permissible noise levels for aircraft in inhabited areas round airports. In this respect Russia is in a more favourable position than any other European country, for she has unlimited space and can site her airports favourably.

STATE STANDARD FOR NOISE

A USSR state standard for 'noise and general safety requirements' has been drafted by the Institute For Labour Safety, which is a first step to establishing legislation aimed at combating environmental pollution. The influence of noise on the human organism and maximum levels for streets, housing areas, flats, shops and hospitals have been determined, and these norms have been given the force of law.

Specially designed noise-level standards are being drawn up for machines in factories, especially rumbling mechanisms such as compressors, ventilation units and mine drills, and there are noise limits for metal-cutting machines, electric motors and tools. The result is that in factories where workers had to communicate with each other by signs, they now converse in normal tones. One example is a section at the Shchelkovo complex near Moscow, which operates looms of the 'epee' type. The role of the shuttle in these machines is now performed by a jet of compressed air which is virtually noiseless.

Every means is found to protect the eardrums of the workers, from mineral acoustic slabs to noise-absorbing earpieces, and workers who think of new and more effective ideas are rewarded.

The walls of homes where people may be affected by noise are soundproofed and the interior walls of prefabricated houses are made thicker. Every city has its noise control commission and notices which read 'Keep Down Noise' are displayed prominently in the Ukranian city of Lvov, an idea that is being copied elsewhere. Noisy vehicles in need of repair are banned, as are noisy loading operations near shops, and the emptying of dustbins in courtyards.

Owners of blaring radios are first warned, then fined, and noise control posts have been set up to report breaches of the law. These measures have reduced street noises considerably. In his book on noise control, published recently by the government in the USSR, Vladimir Chudnev said that with the present level of science and technology it was possible to control noise even in the busiest districts, and he urged that sound-conscious manners should be taught early in homes and nursery schools, where young children should be urged to close doors noiselessly.

ANTI-NOISE EDUCATION

Education to convince people that unnecessary noise is a harmful stimulant is lacking in Britain and America. In the right environment and up to a point, noise can act as a powerful stimulant which enables people to work and play together more efficiently. Every American college, for instance, seems to have its peculiar yell which has the effect of secreting adrenalin in the veins of football players and leads them on to superhuman efforts. But in an enclosed space college yells would eventually do a great deal of harm. The same applies to cheering at soccer and rugger matches.

CANCELLING OUT NOISE

In 1973 Armenian scientists invented a device that cancels noise at its source. It consists of a magnetic tape coupled to a device which records the noise of any piece of mechanism.

When the machine is operated a tape recording is produced in reverse, which interferes with the sound waves and produces silence. The device can be adapted to any kind of noise.

R. J. McCONNELL AND ASSOCIATES

In 1973 R. J. McConnell and Associates, a firm of acoustical engineers in Hertfordshire, published a report which stated that 80 per cent of firms with noisy machinery fail to issue ear protectors to their workers, and those that do issue them say that most workers are reluctant to use them. For this the unions must take much of the blame.

The report implied that 50 per cent (the figure may probably be as high as 80 per cent) of workers in noisy factories are going deaf, and criticized the unions: 'As bodies concerned with the working lives of people trade unions must become more aware of noise as a possible danger to their members, but . . . unions seem to show little concern.' Possibly because they have not been educated to the dangers of noise.

The report states that the sound level in working conditions should not exceed 90 dB for eight hours of any working day. Those who conducted the research say that noise affects not only the ears but other parts of the body as well, especially the internal organs. Though doctors may not realize it, stomach ulcers are sometimes caused by excessive noise at work, but as they seldom know the cause they diagnose in the dark. Heavy engineering, printing and the steel industry produce noise well above the accepted level, but, continues the report, 'few firms are taking steps to rectify this'. A handful of progressive firms, local authorities, architects, planners and even individuals have consulted acoustical experts, always with resulting benefit.

Stock Car and Motorcycle Racing Stadium
McConnells are sometimes called in when noise nuisance affects people in built-up areas. In 1969, when the county

borough of Southend was asked by the owners of a stadium for planning permission to convert part of the area into a racing track for stock cars and speedway racing, they consulted an acoustical expert who submitted an abstruse technical report which the council could not fully understand. So they turned to McConnells, who took 25,000 feet of tape recordings of more than a hundred races at twenty-eight points, and 150,000 sound levels were computed in various ways to achieve objective results. They raised several objections to statements in the report and said that in their opinion the noise created would cause considerable annoyance to nearby residents. A public inquiry followed, and when all the evidence was sifted planning permission was refused.

Nuisance Caused by Vibrations

On another occasion they were commissioned by Bowyer Engineering of Andover, whose office was situated in an industrial area, to track down the cause of heavy vibration which affected their working. Using the latest equipment they discovered that vibration was greatest at certain points of the site and when tape recordings were taken a 'fingerprint' of this vibration was found, which enabled them to track it to its source. The culprit was a large metal-processing machine about half a mile away. When this was pointed out to the owners they agreed to pay 50 per cent of the cost of installing vibration insulators, which cured the nuisance. Bowyer Engineering paid the remainder.

Conversion of an Old Malthouse

In the minds of most people acoustics are associated with theatres and concert halls where clear reception of music and the spoken word is essential. When plans for the Old Malthouse in Ely, which was to be converted to a multi-purpose theatre and concert hall, were drawn up, the architects called in McConnells, who made a thorough study of the problem and recommended that the building be gutted and reconstructed. This was done, with excellent results. Unfortunately, many owners who intend to convert old buildings into concert or lecture halls fail to take expert advice, with lamentable results. Almost invariably they are compelled, at considerable expense, to instal equipment that will produce the right acoustics.

Loss of Hearing and Tinnitus

Yet another example from their fat files of case histories concerns a machinist in a furniture factory where a large multi-purpose wood-working machine had been operating for a number of years. When he first started work the machinist had asked his shop foreman for 'ear defenders' but repeated requests over the years failed to produce them.

When eventually the man's hearing failed and he found it difficult to hear normal speech and was afflicted by a constant buzzing in the head, he consulted his doctor, who diagnosed noise-induced tinnitus, an incurable disease. Tinnitus is a harrowing condition experienced by many who have been exposed to high-level impulsive noises such as artillery or rifle fire.

As the owners disclaimed responsibility the man complained to his union, who called in McConnells. Tests were made to estimate the degree of noise to which he had been exposed, and he also had extensive hospital tests. A report was submitted and the man received compensation.

THE CASE OF DETECTIVE-SUPERINTENDENT McCAFFERTY

In 1975 Detective-Superintendent McCafferty, aged sixty, who for years had been testing firearms as part of his job, found that he was partially deaf, so he sued the Metropolitan Police for compensation. His counsel claimed that deafness was caused because he had to fire thousands of rounds every day in an enclosed space, and he had to be compulsorily retired because he found that his hearing had deteriorated. The premises were not soundproofed in any way and McCafferty was not provided with earmuffs.

NOISE LEVELS INCREASE

Each year more evidence is produced about the destructive effects of noise; especially high levels of modern music. According to two German psychiatrists, performers of loud discordant music become nervous, irritable and aggressive and have headaches, stomach pains and bowel disorders. They found that 75 per cent of musicians in orchestras playing modern works suffered from some form of neurasthenia, whereas only 17 per cent in 'conservative' orchestras were similarly affected. If the trend continues many musicians will end as nervous wrecks.

NOISE IN THE OFFICE

Heavy industry is not the only source of industrial noise. Light industries also produce an immense volume of noise, and anyone not accustomed to it who enters a large open-plan office is hit by a wave of sound. People working in such surroundings can lose as much as 15 per cent in efficiency. In 1974 the Statistical Services Division of the Alfred Marks Bureau questioned 1000 office machine operators and found that most of them complained of headaches or were affected in some other way. Headaches afflicted 46 per cent; backaches 38 per cent; eyestrain 33 per cent; and wrist-ache 15 per cent. In offices that were badly planned or overlooked busy main roads the excessive noise resulted in forms of neuroses; 23 per cent complained of the noise and 42 per cent said it impaired their efficiency.

NOISE IN THE HOME

Nor are housewives immune from the dangers of noise, for the modern home is filled with contraptions that add to it: vacuum cleaner, electric whisk, mixer and juicer, fridge that cuts itself off and comes on with a bump, hairdrier, fanheater, coffee grinder, radio, TV and stereo. Many people keep the radio or TV on all the time, even when not listening or viewing, and, more often than not, much too loudly. Then they wonder why at the end of the day they feel worn out. Or slightly deaf, for if they have small children who need correction they have to shout in order to be heard above the radio. Sunday afternoons and holidays are often ruined by neighbouring lawnmowers, which are invariably in use when one is reading or resting.

A REASONABLE LIMIT OF NOISE

People are affected differently by noise. Some seem almost oblivious to noise that is unbearable to others. Much depends on the sensitivity of the listener. Mozart's nerves were shattered by the blast of a trumpet, yet many play the trumpet for pleasure. I was trained as an engineer and went through the main departments of a big railway works to gain experience. Six months in the boiler shop with the constant riveting and clattering of hammers so deadened my hearing that it took me months to recover. The foreman was almost completely deaf, and one had to yell at him to make him hear. Conversation carried on by shouting is in itself fatiguing. Many who worked in the shop were either partly or completely deaf. In the power station noise was considerable but bearable, as it was of an even intensity and the droning of the alternators had a soporific effect. When I emerged from the building I was met with 'a blast of silence'.

It is difficult, therefore, to lay down an absolute set of standards for noise, for some revel in noise that makes others ill. A few days in the Bombay Stock Exchange, for instance, where all shout at the tops of their voices, would destroy the sanity of the average man.

In 1965 the Noise Abatement Society and the Medical Research Council disagreed on the subject of industrial noise and occupational deafness. In their Report the Council suggested that prolonged noise below 95 decibels did not impair working efficiency, but when Mr John Connell of the NAS invited Mr Cawthorn of the MRC to submit to a lengthy test under working conditions where noise registered 94 decibels – the equivalent of a dozen motorcycles all revving at once – he very sensibly declined.

COLONEL GROGNOT'S EXPERIMENT

He must have known about the test carried out by Colonel Grognot, a French army doctor, who subjected 500 men to 90 decibels of sound for fifteen minutes, approximately the volume of sound one would hear if standing within a foot of a heavy diesel engine revving up. The men were then tested and were found to have swollen arteries. Their hearts were also affected and they were deaf for two hours. Even more significant, 75 per cent suffered from colour blindness and 70 per cent had double margin of error in vision. If traffic noise grows much worse the roar might affect motorists in much the same way, and the resulting increase in accidents could be frightening.

Those who live in the vicinity of airports – there are 40,000 round Heathrow – find the noise intolerable and suffer from sleeplessness. No one has estimated how much this has cost in efficiency and health.

CASUALTIES OF THE INDUSTRIAL AGE

Hundreds of thousands are rendered partly deaf by machines in factories, offices, homes and discotheques. A Harley Street specialist said recently: 'Within the past year I have treated four or five people in their early twenties for serious deafness – and they have all been associated with terribly noisy bands. One was a discotheque manager. Ten years ago one would hardly see people with this sort of hearing loss.'

The pop group singer Phil Lynott, vocalist of the Thin

Lizzy group, told a reporter: 'I've been told by a specialist to pack it in. I kept waking up in the morning with a piercing whine in my ears. I may have to think again if I find my hearing is completely in jeopardy.'*

THE DANGER OF POP MUSIC

In America, the home of jazz and other types of noisy music, people are afflicted to a greater degree than in Britain. Mr Frederick Day, an audiologist in New London, Connecticut, said that the noise in the local discotheque was 110 decibels – louder than that made by a jet plane! This battering of the eardrums hour after hour causes the bones in the ear to thicken and plays havoc with the nervous system.

In *A Pilot Study on the Effects of Pop Group Music On Hearing* † a group of researchers said that the spectra of pop music had levels in the order of 110 dB (A), which greatly exceed the tolerable limits set out in the Federal Register.

Lebo and Oliphant made measurements for both rock and fortissimo symphonic music and found that whereas symphonic music is well below damage risk levels, rock is not. What is more, fortissimo symphonic music is not played hour after hour, or even for long periods, whereas rock is. The damage from rock extends over a wide range of frequencies from about 500 Hz to 4000 Hz.

The *New Scientist* stated: 'Even two hours at 110 decibels – the normal rate of exposure during rock sessions – will cause loss of hearing in about 16 per cent of young people.' This loss is temporary, lasting about an hour, but if repeated for weeks or months as is the case with those who frequent discotheques, permanent deafness is often the result. This may not be apparent at first, but the *British Medical Journal* says: 'It is possible

---

* *Daily Mail*: 9 September 1973.

† C. G. Rice, J. B. Ayley, B. Bartlett, W. Bedford, W. Gregory and G. Hallam.

to listen to music in this way in such shattering volume that the inner ear is damaged.'

THE EAR – A DELICATE INSTRUMENT

Because the hearing apparatus is easily damaged, Nature has placed it deep in the skull. Few mothers realize, however, that kissing a baby on the open ear may produce deafness. Not long ago a driving instructor in Neuilly, France, ruptured the eardrum of a pretty pupil when at the close of a lesson he exclaimed: 'Well done, chérie!' and planted a full-blown kiss on her ear. A magistrate held him guilty of assault and awarded the girl damages.

There are also people in professions other than industry who risk deafness: skin divers, high divers, parachutists, tunnellers, and those 'sportsmen' who each August bang off 1000 rounds or more at inoffensive grouse.

DR CHARLES WARREN

The vibrations from noise increase each year in volume and intensity. A drill or a ram operating outside an office window or a private dwelling can drive those inside to distraction. Dr Warren, an ear specialist, said forty years ago that the eardrums of many of his patients were thickening; the small bones inside the ear were stiffening and losing movement, and the cartilage around the aural windows was also thickening. In extreme cases the hearing nerves became exhausted and eventually failed to transmit vibration. The result was deafness.

SIR WALTER FERGUSSON HANNAY

In 1960 Sir Walter Fergusson Hannay, chairman of the Noise Abatement Society, addressing women Public Health Officers at an Association meeting in London, said that if the volume of noise continued to grow: 'Britain might become a race of shouting maniacs ... If the general noisy conditions of everyday life continue it is not inconceivable that we shall all become increasingly deaf and have to shout at one another if our normal conversational gambits are to be heard by those to whom we speak.' He added that it was the hypersensitive, so commonly labelled neurotic and hypochondriac, who were the creators and constructive workers responsible for making modern civilization the wonder it was.

Sir Walter divided people into three groups: the insensitive who are scarcely affected by, and usually make the most noise; the sensitive, who are troubled by it but manage to adjust themselves; and the hypersensitive, who are shattered by noise and suffer most of all.

DEAFNESS

Deafness is Nature's defence against a complete breakdown in health. If the victim does not become deaf the nervous system will eventually become affected, and in the case of the hypersensitive a breakdown in health occurs long before deafness sets in.

Noise acts like a drug. There is no condition to which the body so quickly adjusts itself, and there lies its deadliness. Vibrations produced by noise can exhilarate, especially the young, who seem to revel in it. If the elderly hark back they will be astonished and shocked by the excessive noise they created. Apparently, as we age our auditory apparatus grows more sensitive and we dislike noise more and more. The philosopher Schopenhauer hated noise and believed that most of the misfortunes of the world could be attributed to it. He was convinced that the brains of noise-makers were of very coarse quality and positive that the Germans, the rowdiest people in Europe, would come to a sticky end. They have certainly disturbed the peace of Europe twice within the last sixty years.

DEGREES OF DEAFNESS

Deafness is one of the most difficult conditions to define, for it ranges from stone-deafness to psychological deafness. There are also those who are tone-deaf, which is a misfortune but not a disease. The psychologically deaf are usually found among relatives whose faces remain blank when asked to do a job in the house, such as washing up, painting walls, or mowing the lawn, but whose hearing is inconveniently keen when a comment is whispered that they are not supposed to hear.

TONE-DEAFNESS

The tone-deaf are to be pitied, for they miss much beauty and cannot appreciate great music, which just seems noise to them. George II, for instance, could not distinguish one note from another. He stood up when the 'Hallelujah Chorus' was played, under the impression that it was the national anthem, and ever since audiences have done likewise. Now it has become a tradition.

Apparently tone-deafness can be cured. Professor A. N. Leontyev, of the Moscow Academy of Sciences, claims to have devised a method of teaching the tone-deaf to sing in tune and maintains that an ear for music can be developed.

NOISE DESTROYS

The way in which noise affects people differs, but in every instance, even though they may not realize it, noise causes fatigue and fatigue causes concentration to falter. According to Dr Keith Jolles, consultant in motoring medicine, noisy stereo music in cars makes drivers 'noise drunk' and unable to cope with traffic problems and hazards. 'These new stereo and quadraphone outfits,' he says, 'which bombard the driver with sound from all round him can cause extreme fatigue if played too loudly; but properly used, stereo music can prevent fatigue.' Most young people play it too loudly.

Once hooked, noise becomes a drug they must have, and the owner of a large garage told an investigator: 'I have seen young drivers buying these cartridges at £2 a time when they should be spending the money on new tyres.'

DRIVERS AND INFRASOUND

Till recently no one has worried about the dangers of low-frequency or infrasounds, as they are called, to motorists. Tests carried out by the British Acoustical Society at the University of Salford in 1971 showed that cars and lorries travelling at sustained high speeds produce intense levels of low-frequency noise which has the same effect on drivers as heavy drinking. Alertness and efficiency are impaired, the balance mechanism in the ears becomes disturbed, a sense of euphoria overcomes them, they become reckless and their reactions are slowed by as much as 30 per cent. Some drivers have wandered across the central strip on the road with little regard to oncoming traffic. How many deaths have been caused by this condition will never be known, but many a head-on crash must have resulted.

Infrasound is noise with a frequency below 32 vibrations a second (or three octaves below middle C) and can be produced by fast cars, trains, planes and oil-fired boilers. Dr Tempest of Salford University said that cars travelling at high speeds on motorways were a particular menace, for with windows closed most cars produce infrasounds around or greater than 100 dB, but with windows open even a few inches the levels shoot up to 110 or even 120 dB, causing an imbalance of the hearing mechanism, dizziness and swaying movements of the body, all of which have a marked effect on driving efficiency and safety.

NOISE TESTS

In 1973 monkeys were subjected to noise tests at the University of Wisconsin and all displayed symptoms of stress and extreme fatigue. There is little need to test monkeys when humans are available. British workers assembling transistor sets under microscopes, which requires intense concentration, suffered losses of efficiency as high as 70 per cent because they worked next door to a milling plant which created a great deal of noise.

Tests carried out in an electronics factory near London where noisy conditions existed revealed that 110 workers each made sixty mistakes in twenty-four hours. When transferred to quieter surroundings the number of mistakes fell to only seven in the same period.

Welsh workers exposed to the terrific roar of oxygen-fired furnaces have been found to suffer bouts of nausea, giving rise to extraordinary errors in the reading of gauges. When they were equipped with earmuffs their efficiency increased dramatically.

Diesel locomotives create a high level of noise which reverberates sickeningly when they stand in enclosed main line stations – a noise that has made many a hypersensitive person waiting in a carriage near the engine become ill with emotional distress. What effect it has on the concentration of the drivers can only be imagined. Such noise must also reduce the efficiency of the station staff who are subjected to it for as long as they are on duty.

That noise can have a shattering effect on people was proved by Dr P. J. T. Challen and Dr H. E. Hickish of the Slough Industrial Health Service when in 1960 they embarked on a series of tests. Dr Hickish, an occupational hygiene engineer, listened to an electric saw for three and a half hours, during which time his hearing deteriorated rapidly and it took him two days to recover. The effect on the hearing of men who work with electric saws for a livelihood must be shattering. Those who are immune must be extremely insensitive, otherwise they could not stand the racket, though after a while their eardrums become inured to it. Even so, it must have a harmful effect on the nervous system.

NOISE COUPLED WITH VIBRATION

Noise is not the only destructive force. Men who work with noisy machines that vibrate from 40 to 140 times a minute – road drills, lightweight chainsaws and riveters – also suffer. Even driving long distances in a noisy truck that rattles and bumps can be very exhausting. A symptom known as 'Dead Hand' or 'White Fingers' sets in, and is known technically as Vibration Syndrome. The medical name is Raynaud's Phenomenon, which is now listed as an industrial disease for which compensation may be claimed. The symptoms are numbness, as if the hands have been exposed to intense cold for long periods. At first the victim notices that his hands are white and numb and remain clumsy after work has finished.

Soon after the symptoms were first noticed the Transport and General Workers' Union reported 25 cases in Liverpool, Norwich and Scotland. One man complained that he was rendered sexually impotent. Another said that when he got home his car had a flat tyre but his hands were so numb that he could not change the wheel. A third went to a soccer match after work, but when he slipped a hand into a pocket to extract the entrance money his fingers could not feel it, which made him look foolish as he held up the queue. A fourth visited the seaside on a scorching day but could not dress himself after a dip and his wife was forced to help him change his trunks. A fifth bought a motorcycle but had to sell it for less than half the price he paid because his hands had lost all sense of feeling, which nearly caused him to have an accident. A sixth who went fishing was incapable of handling his reel.

When claims for compensation for this disability mounted rapidly the authorities grew alarmed, and a group led by Dr William Taylor of the Department of Occupational Medicine at Dundee University began studying the new disease and in a short time advised modifications to all vibrating machinery. They also encouraged the design of machinery that did not vibrate.

The first successful action for damages by a victim of Raynaud's Phenomenon was brought by Mr James Lambert of Luton, who worked on a Vauxhall assembly line. His counsel, Mr Alan Lipfriend, said that the disease prevented him from gardening, walking in winter and going swimming with his daughters. Medical evidence was produced which stated that he was in danger of contracting gangrene, though this was disputed. The company admitted a degree of liability, however, and Mr Lambert was awarded £1 500 damages, with costs.*

The hazards of noise increase disproportionately each year. Cars devour distance and are doubtless a wonderful invention, but they make life a hell for all who live too near our motorways, and the government pays out millions of pounds in compensation to householders to make their dwellings soundproof. In 1972 they paid 75 per cent towards the cost of acquiring houses in the London borough of Tower Hamlets to residents whose lives had been rendered intolerable. Their former homes stood 30 feet from a six-line elevated approach to the Blackwall Tunnel, and they suffered from noise, intense vibration and visual intrusion.

Others elsewhere, similarly affected, have not always been so fortunate.

NEIGHBOURLY NOISE

One type of noise from which people all over the country suffer is the clang of church bells. No one objects to the gentle tolling of bells which summon the godly to worship, though in an age when everyone has a watch, every home one or more clocks, and when the time may be had from radio or TV, or by dialling TIM, church bells seem an anachronism. No one objects to the tolling of bells for a few seconds, and if one lives in cities like Oxford and Cambridge where chimes are played

* *Daily Mail*: 26 May 1973.

hourly or at shorter intervals, one grows accustomed to them. It is quite another thing to have to listen to the senseless and antisocial marathon performances of bellringers (an insensitive tribe) in built-up areas. Anyone forced to listen to the ringing of peals (a peal is the ringing on seven bells of 5040 changes; a lesser number being a 'touch') can be forgiven if he contemplates mayhem or even murder, and in an age so filled with noise, such an activity is indefensible. Being forced to listen to 'peals' can send a hypersensitive person over the edge, for the listener is an involuntary prisoner.

DEAFNESS IS AN INDUSTRIAL DISEASE

Not until 1971 was deafness recognized legally as an industrial disease which entitled the victim to compensation. The first to win a claim was Mr Frank R. Berry of Charlton, London. He told the court that he worked in 'an inferno of noise', which was tested and found to be between 115 and 120 decibels. When he first entered the employ of Stone Manganese and Marine Ltd, fourteen years previously, the noise 'frightened the life' out of him, and a witness stated that the noise was on the threshold of pain. His employers did not insist on earmuffs being worn and they were not supplied till 1966. Mr Justice Ashworth in giving judgement and awarding him £1500 said that had his action been brought three years earlier he would have given him £2500.

FACTORY NOISE

In the past one could set up a factory anywhere and make as much noise as possible without fear of prosecution, but today those who live adjacent to factories enjoy a measure of protection. In 1964 four householders took out an action against Mining Supplies Ltd, manufacturers of coal cutting machinery at Orksey. They complained that over a long period they had been disturbed during weekdays and sometimes on Sundays by hammering and other noises. The factory had caused them many sleepless nights. Mr Justice Flint, sitting at Doncaster County Court, awarded each of the plaintiffs £50 and costs, and made an injunction restraining the firm from allowing noise to issue from its machinery and lorries between the hours of 7 pm and 7 am, and one more battle against noise had been won.

Residents in close proximity of factories are within their rights to complain if noise is excessive after certain hours and disturbs their sleep, and this applies to places of entertainment as well. In 1976 the owners of the Welcome Inn, Marton, Blackpool, were fined £400 because a brass band playing in their gardens registered noise as loud as piledriving equipment. They were charged under the new Control of Pollution Act.

There are no hard-and-fast rules as to what is too much noise. Mr Justice Goff stated in the High Court in 1971 when granting an injunction to a householder: 'The question is whether the evidence as a whole establishes an actionable nuisance according to ordinary notions of comfort.' Which allows considerable latitude.

THE CASE OF MISS BRAGGINS

In June 1958 Mrs Margaret Gordon sued her nextdoor neighbour Miss Braggins, a Doctor of Music and a Master of Arts, because she practised scales and arpeggios and sometimes emitted noises 'like a hunted animal'.

Her counsel, Mr Ashe Lincoln, told the court that 'baying, wailing, warbling and hooting sounds' emerged from Miss Braggins' flat, but Miss Braggins said that the sounds came from a tape recorder and not from her. Mr Justice Plowman ruled that a tape recorder is a musical instrument and should not be played loudly outside permitted hours, and Miss Braggins was ordered to stop annoying her neighbours.

SARAH BERNSTEIN

Mrs Sarah Bernstein lived in a flat and made the lives of neighbours above and below her miserable because she insisted that, having paid her TV licence fee, she was entitled to play that instrument as loudly as she pleased. In this respect Mr David Hopkin, the presiding magistrate, had different ideas. He ordered her to pay £15, and because she was seventy-one years of age bound her over to keep the peace and remanded her for medical and psychiatric treatment.

THE MUSICAL LEVINGTONS

The Levingtons of Wimbledon are a music-loving family. Their home orchestra, consisting of trumpet, clarinet, viola, violin and piano, caused much annoyance to the Parsons, who lived in the flat above them, and despite protests they continued blasting away. Eventually they were taken to court, and after a three-day hearing which cost the Levingtons £2000 Mr Justice Donaldson severely restricted the days and hours during which they could practise, though they were free to play whenever the Parsons were away from home.

THE NOISE ABATEMENT SOCIETY

The excessively noisy insist on their rights without considering the rights of others, and it was for the protection from the battering of sound vibrations that the Noise Abatement Society was formed. In 1973 Mr Geoffrey Rippon, Minister for the Environment, proposed legal measures to control noise, with fines of up to £400, plus £100 a day for continuing offences. The heads of the TUC, who were consulted by the Ministry, said that the penalties were not severe enough, and new legislation is pending. Nevertheless, under the Recurring Nuisances Act of 1969 a number of inconsiderate people who held noisy parties well after midnight have been prosecuted by various local authorities, and when the new Act is on the Statute Book the teeth of the law will bite even harder. If it does the nation will benefit vastly, for not long ago Mr Rupert Taylor, chairman of the Noise Monitoring Group of the government's Noise Advisory Council, said: 'About a million people risk having their hearing permanently damaged all the time they are at work.' Excessive noise is costing the nation £2,000,000,000 a year in decreased efficiency.

THE EXAMPLE OF BELGIUM

In Britain the authorities make all the right noises but are reluctant to pass laws lest the freedom of individuals is restricted. Unfortunately advice and good example is not enough. The Belgians realize this as far as noise is concerned and under a new law all who make too much noise – organ grinders, disco owners, possessors of hi-fi equipment and jukeboxes – will have to pay more attention to the rights of others. The penalty for a first offence is up to one month in prison or a fine of from £30 to £300, or both. Karel Poma, Secretary of State for the Environment, explained: 'Noise constitutes a menace for the well-being of all mankind and to public health in all its aspects. Exposure to high levels can be harmful both physically and mentally.' The law about noise, he added, was meant to protect teenagers and customers of licensed premises against 'unreasonable' levels at which music is played, and jukeboxes and other musical installations will not be allowed to play at above 90 decibels at source. Such establishments must also be soundproofed so that the level of noise outside does not exceed five decibels.

A similar law is badly needed in Britain, and the police must be enabled to carry it out. Such laws are seldom enforced. The law about litter, for instance, which carries a fine of £10, is seldom put into operation, and litter is scattered about the countryside even where bins of ample size are provided.

PREVENTION OF DEAFNESS

Those who live in an environment free from industrial noise have the keenest hearing. Dr Rosen of the Mount Sinai Hospital, New York, and four of his colleagues, made a study of noise in relation to hearing losses and coronary disease. They found that the primitive Mabaan tribe who live in south-east Sudan, in an environment virtually free from noise, do not know the meaning of coronary disease or atherosclerosis. The hearing of the Mabaans from the ages of ten to seventy is significantly more acute than that of city dwellers and far more so than Europeans and Americans. This is true of others who live remote from civilization, such as the Aborigines of Australia. If you wish to prevent deafness, or improve your hearing, try to find a job, or live, in a quieter atmosphere.

Other Causes of Deafness
Diet also has a considerable bearing on hearing. A diet stodgy with starch and heavy meat meals is likely to cause hardness of hearing in middle age, and so is a lack of vitamins. It has been proved that deafness is one of the symptoms of pellagra and beri-beri, which are caused by a lack of the B-complex vitamins. Tinnitus, said by some doctors to be incurable, is brought about by the decay of the auditory nerves, and many cases have been relieved by larger doses of vitamin C. It is a harrowing disease and can make life miserable.

Vitamin A is also of value in tinnitus and progressive deafness. Dr H. W. Bau and Dr L. Savitt have cured patients suffering from both conditions by injecting them with 50,000 units of vitamin A daily.

A short fast of from one to three days is the best way to cure deafness caused by heavy colds, and a longer fast of up to seven days will usually cure all forms of deafness, except those where the hearing mechanism is damaged.

Chiropractic for Deafness
Ever since Daniel David Palmer * cured Harvey Lillard, a jan-

---

* D. D. Palmer of Davenport, Iowa, founder of chiropractic.

itor who suffered from stone-deafness, by applying a sharp thrust to a vertebra, chiropractors and osteopaths have had remarkable successes in curing deafness. Acupuncturists also claim to cure most forms of deafness.

Temporary deafness can be caused by blowing the nose the wrong way, and children with heavy colds should be advised not to nip one nostril as they blow violently through the other as this produces a back pressure which is likely to affect the Eustachian tubes which run from the middle ear to the back of the throat, though in normal health the danger is slight.

2

Ultrasonics

AMERICA – PIONEER IN ULTRASONICS RESEARCH

America, the most scientific-minded nation, has always been in the forefront of ultrasonics research. In the early 1930s sound waves above the limits of human audibility were used in America to mix oil and water into a homogeneous liquid, and mercury and water, which had never been mixed before, into a dirty-looking emulsion. By the use of ultrasonics eggs were cooked without raising their temperature; and raw eggs were kept fresh for months; and the decay of many vegetables, fruit and other edibles was also retarded.

Almost simultaneously Dr Rudolph Pohlmann of the Berlin Institute announced that high-frequency sound had uses in medicine. These inaudible vibrations were used to kill sea-weed, fish, frogs and other forms of life. When exposed to ultrasound their cells seemed to swell and burst, causing death. He found, however, that this did not happen to the red corpuscles of the blood as long as they remained in their natural serum.

It occurred to him that the swollen cells would absorb more foreign substances, so he coated frogs with blue pigment and exposed them to ultrasonics. They did not die but the dye was driven in as if they had been tattooed. In time the frogs recovered their natural colour.

He reasoned that if dyes can be forced into living cells, chemicals which would either heal or kill could also be forced into cells. By turning the sound on and off at intervals he found it was possible to massage the cells below the skin, so he massaged himself and his assistants, relieving them of sciatica and neuralgia, and eventually of forms of rheumatism.

Pohlmann and others working in the same field discovered that germs which resisted boiling, freezing and pasteurizing succumbed to radiation of high-frequency waves. In chemical experiments ultrasonic waves act as a catalyst* and can break down starch into dextrin, generate acetylene from vegetable oils, break apart some substances and combine others.

They discovered that supersonic waves travel slightly faster than audible sounds and their wave lengths shorten as the frequency increases. Sixteen-cycle sound has a distance of 21 feet between crests; 16,000 cycle sound measures a quarter inch between crests; and sound vibrating at 1,000.000 cycles a second has waves with crests only one seventy-fifth of an inch apart.

Pioneers were amazed at the tricks they could play with their new toy. They could make water appear to boil violently without the temperature rising above that of the room, and liquid hump itself into a hillock and defy gravity. They made chips of wood burst into flames without applying heat to them, and crumbled glass into powder. There seemed to be no limit to their new-found power.

DR LESLIE CHALMERS

Dr Leslie Chalmers and Dr Newton Gaines of Boston impregnated fluid with microbes and subjected them to hammer

---

* An agent which alters the rate at which a chemical reaction occurs but is in itself unchanged at the end of the reaction.

blows of supersonic vibrations which tore the walls of the germs to shreds, precipitating them to the bottom, leaving their anti-bodies unharmed in the liquid. The success of their experiments opened up many possibilities in the field of medicine. They found that a quartz crystal half an inch thick developed an acceleration or 'shaking-up force' ten thousand times as powerful as that of gravity. If, for instance, a glass bottle is dropped on a hard surface the pull of gravity exercises a force powerful enough to smash it to splinters, but supersonic waves exercise a force ten thousand times as strong.

EXPERIMENTS WITH MILK

Milk has a number of chemical compounds floating in it in lumps. The curd, for instance, which is distinct from the whey, makes it difficult for some people to digest milk. Supersonic waves pulverize all the lumps into curd, soften and homogenize them with the whey so that they are easily digested, and any bacteria lurking in the milk are destroyed. This is unfortunate, as most of the bacteria in milk are harmless or even beneficial. Chalmers and Gaines poured a quantity of milk polluted by micro-organisms into a flask and subjected it to infrasound, and in forty minutes 96 per cent were destroyed. They then continued till total destruction was achieved, after which they designed a machine called a 'soniser' capable of dealing with 1500 gallons an hour.

DR OSCAR BRUNLER

Probably the first physician in Britain to treat the sick with vibrations was Dr Oscar Brunler, of London. In 1934 a man suffering from a tropical skin disease, who had failed to gain the slightest relief though he had made the round of hospitals and specialists, called on him in desperation. Brunler first treated him with light, which gave him considerable relief but did not cure; then with air currents of a certain intensity; finally with ultrasonics till he was completely cured.

'Every person,' explained Brunler, 'has a tone which is always present in the voice and it is a simple matter to find its frequency. One method is to light a number of gas jets and watch them closely. When the patient speaks one of them "sings". Once the "tone" has been determined, a corresponding note in the vibratory scale will soon cure him.'

This method of applying the 'tone' can be varied: it can be pitched at an octave high enough to be inaudible to the patient, who can sleep while being treated.

THE KEYNOTE

All matter, living and inanimate, has a keynote. Claude Bragdon the architect, who practised yoga, invited the opera singer Marie Russak to the New York Central Station which he had designed, before it was open to the public. 'As she stood in the gallery,' says Bragdon, 'she ran up the notes of the diatonic scale in her rich, powerful voice. At the utterance of a certain note the entire room seemed to become a great resonance chamber, reinforcing the tone with a volume of sound so great as to be almost overpowering. The walls, ceiling and the entire building seemed to shout aloud.

' "There!" cried the singer as the sound died away in overtones. "Now your building has found its keynote – it's alive!" '

CHARLES KELLOGG

For years the naturalist Charles Kellogg experimented with sound to find out what effect it had on plants. He found that sound could extinguish flames and wondered whether it could be used for fire-fighting.

In 1926 in the Palace Theatre, New York, he gave a demonstration to a group of firemen, by passing a bow like that used on a gigantic violin swiftly across an aluminium tuning fork, producing a screech like an intense radio static. Instantly a gas jet two feet high in a hollow glass tube, subsided to a height of 6 inches and dwindled to a spluttering flame. When the bow was passed across the tuning fork once again another screech was produced and the light was extinguished.

Incidentally, architects always have to take into account the resonant frequency of skyscrapers, which might set them vibrating destructively in a high wind.

ECHOES

Vibrations produce many curious effects, some of which baffle scientists. Among the most baffling are echoes. In Barisal, part of Bangladesh, the sound of heavy and prolonged artillery fire is often heard though there is no artillery within 100 miles or more, and no one has yet discovered why these 'Barisal guns', as they are called, are heard.

In Oxfordshire there is a valley where a pistol shot can be heard echoing as many as twenty times, and a hammer blow on the main pier of the Menai Suspension Bridge is returned in a series of staccato reports from each of its crossbeams through its 576 feet.

Thousands during the war experienced the peculiarities of blast when those near the explosion were untouched but buildings hundreds of yards away were demolished. When the Simplon Tunnel was being driven through the Alps there was an occasion when tons of dynamite were exploded, the blast of which was heard by peasants more than 20 miles away though those in villages in between heard nothing. The blast was also heard 100 miles to the north, in Germany! Why had the vibrations made two distinct jumps? The Swiss Meteorological Institute said that the echo heard in Germany was a 'mirror echo', caused by the vibrations travelling upwards till they reached heavy cloud formations 50 miles to the north, and then being reflected back to earth.

PECULIARITIES OF SOUND VIBRATIONS

If one visits a certain ancient tomb on the Roman Campagna and speaks an entire hexameter verse, the echo will wait till the speaker has finished and then repeat it. For this to happen there must be a reflector at least half a mile away, but why some vibrations are returned in whispers and others in bangs cannot be explained. If, for instance, a sheet of cellophane is crumpled in a famous quarried grotto known as the Ear of Dionysius in Sicily, the echo returns like the sound of a stream of machinegun bullets.

There are also harmonic echoes. One at the Gap of Dunloe, near the Lakes of Killarney, is caused by blowing a bugle, though the note returns an octave higher and provides a harmonious accompaniment to a bugle call.

SOUND SPECTRUM

It is common knowledge that prisms break up light into its component colours, but few people know that some echoes also break up sound in a similar way. In Bighorn Canyon, Southern Montana, the roar of a rushing river echoes in a certain section between cliffs into a howl like a police siren, starting on a high note and sweeping down into a bass note. On the Saddleback Mountain in Maine, the most hideous discord, such as an Indian war whoop or a raucous college yell, returns in sweet melodious notes.

WHISPERING GALLERIES

Scattered throughout the world are many whispering galleries, one of the best known being that in the dome of St Paul's, London. A mere whisper will creep across and can be heard distinctly 102 feet on the other side. In Syracuse there is a prison built by the tyrant Dionysius, into which enemies who plotted against him were thrown. What they did not realize is that their muted secrets could be heard clearly at the top of the 120-foot tower where his agents lay in hiding.

ULTRASONICS IN MEDICINE

Many of the secrets of vibrations have been harnessed by the medical profession who, dubious at first, were impressed when results were favourable. Their caution was justified as charlatans jumped on the bandwagon and did a great deal of harm. Gradually as they were trained to use ultrasonics they realized its potentialities. In 1963 Dr Robert Cochrane, leprosy consultant to the Ministry of Health and the American Mission for Leprosy, sent a patient to St George's Hospital, Tooting, with legs so dreadfully ulcerated that it was thought amputation alone could save her life. Fortunately they called in Mr Leonard Norman, a Wimpole Street physiotherapist, who agreed to treat her with ultrasonic vibrations, which he did without charge. After forty-six treatments she was cured.

As Lord Hailsham, Minister of Health at the time, complained that Britain lagged behind many poorer countries in the use of ultrasonic machines, Mr Norman sent him a book he had written on the subject, which was passed on to his advisers. Their reply was that ultrasonic treatment was of no value whatever![*]

According to Mr Norman there were some five hundred ultrasonic machines in Britain, but most of them unused because there were not enough skilled men to operate them. 'The United Kingdom,' he said, 'is the only major nation in the world where ultrasonic therapy is not freely available to patients.' The position has changed since then and it is now used in the treatment of many diseases, especially varicose veins.

DIAGNOSIS BY ULTRASONICS

Ultrasonics is a specialized field and those who labour in it

[*] *Observer*: 22 September 1963.

often have to design entirely new apparatus as they feel their way. As it is difficult to transmit very high-frequency waves through air, and even more difficult to pass them into liquids or solids and vice versa, experiments are confined to passing waves having millions of cycles rather than thousands into liquids and solids, and their use in diagnosing disease has been found invaluable.

In Russia they found that ultrasonics give far more information than X-rays. They make it possible, for instance, to look inside the eye, and determine the anomalies of the crystalline lens.

Beams reflected from the surface of a tumour enable the physician to detect malignant tumours in the organism at a much earlier stage, and so combat the disease successfully.

Accurate diagnosis is the key to successful cures. During a conference in Moscow on 30 June 1973, Professor Irinia Golyamina, head of the laboratory of the Moscow Acoustics Institute, said that one of the most promising trends in ultrasonics was the use it had in diagnostics. In heart disease it gives a picture of the heart in any phase, at the moment of constriction or relaxation. The image obtained is clear and can be photographed, and if the physician has full information on the condition of the heart, its ventricles and vessels, he can not only give a correct diagnosis but take a decision either to operate or give therapeutic treatment.

ULTRASOUND IN THE HEALING OF INJURIES

In May 1970 Professor Mstislav Volkov, director of the Central Institute of Traumatology and Orthopaedics, stated that ultrasound had been used in dozens of operations to join bones and eliminate tumours. In the case of a five-year-old girl with a gigantic tumour of the left radial bone, an operation was performed. The tumour had so emaciated the tissue that the bone had broken and the wrist hung lifelessly. The tumour was removed and the defect filled in with a welded conglomerate. *In a week* the wound had healed and the child was able to move her fingers freely. A similar operation was carried out on a patient with a tumour on the upper third of a broken shoulder bone, equally successfully.

Altogether more than four hundred operations involving the welding of bones by ultrasonic surgery were performed on animals before the method was used in clinics.

Engineers collaborating with surgeons proposed the use of a very strong plastic as an intermediary material, to act as a kind of solder between welded bone fractures, for without such protection bone would instantly be charred by ultrasound.

ULTRASOUND AS A PAINKILLER

Professor Volkov said that in physiotherapy ultrasound was often used to remove pain, and is now used as a painkiller in surgery after operations, for it is found that on the day following surgery most patients so treated do not feel any pain at all.

ULTRASOUND FOR CUTTING AND WELDING BONE TISSUE

On 25 August 1971 Academician Boris Petrovsky told an International Congress of Surgeons in Moscow that ultrasound had been used with great success in cutting and welding bone tissue, and in particular in traumatology, orthopaedy and chest surgery. Far less injury was inflicted when cutting with ultrasound than with an electric saw. The ultrasonic method was almost bloodless, bone fragments knitted much faster, and no pain was felt for two or three days after operations.

'Welding' is a new term in medicine and means precisely what it says. Bone shavings are deposited in the spaces between bones, pasted with a special glue and then 'ironed out' with a wave guide, forming a strong joint. In 1971 more than five hundred operations were carried out by a method of bone welding developed by Professor G. A. Nikolayev of the Bauman Technical School in Moscow, experimenting on animals. When these were successful thirty adults and children were similarly treated by Professor V. Polyakov at the Union Central Institute of Advanced Medical Training.

TONSILLITIS CURED BY ULTRASOUND

In 1972 a device for curing tonsillitis, known as LOR-IA was exhibited at the USSR Economic Exhibition in Moscow. It was based on the triple effect of ultrasound.

First, waves are directed on to the tonsils, giving them vibrational massage which causes an intense flow of blood and improves the organism's capacity to combat infection. The waves have a secondary thermal effect, heating tissue around the tonsils. Finally, they kill pain, which makes tonsillectomy so dreaded. The treatment, which is not given to bedridden patients, consists of ten sessions, and patients who are seriously ill can undergo a second course.

ULTRASONIC MASSAGE

Originally the most widely used application of ultrasound was massage, which was used as a substitute for hands where patients had suffered fractures or other injuries. In Britain the method became obsolete when it was realized that the same results could be produced by medical diathermy and short-wave therapy. Ultrasonics have many uses in other diseases, however, and new ones are being developed almost every year.

RHEUMATISM

It was thought at first that ultrasound was the answer to rheumatism and some clinicians found it of the utmost value. Others, curiously enough, said it was useless. The reason remains a mystery.

SURGERY

Every tissue of the body can be irradiated by ultrasound, but it has been found that its value so far as a destructive agent is confined almost entirely to the nervous system. This is because nerve tissue, particularly the myelinated fibres of the brain, spinal cord and peripheral nerves show exceptional susceptibility to sound.

All methods of destroying nerve tissue suffer from the objection that they affect vessels more than nerve tissue; it is impossible, therefore, to destroy nerve tissue without risking damage to an artery which supplies blood to tissue outside the target area.

Ultrasound is of immense value in neuro-surgery, such as the removal of part of the brain in Parkinson's disease (pallidectomy), which stops tremors, and in parts of the very front of the brain (leucotomy) where patients suffer from abnormal anxiety states.

MÉNIÈRE'S DISEASE

This is a comparatively rare disease, the cause of which is unknown. There is progressive deterioration in the function of the Eighth or Acoustic Nerve. The symptoms are giddiness, tinnitus and tension within the ear. Utrasonic treatment has had great success and it is only when the tension within the ear has disappeared that the patient is aware he had it.

PITUITARY IRRADIATION

Often the removal of this gland by ultrasound has a significant effect on cancer of the organs, particularly of the breast, ovary and uterus. It also benefits, even if it does not always cure, patients with diabetes retinitus, a rare complication of diabetes which leads to complete blindness. Tumours of the pituitary can also be treated by ultrasound.

In ophthalmic surgery ultrasound is invaluable in detecting tumours at the back of the eye, but it cannot compare with lasers in surgery of detachments of the retina.

DENTISTRY

Most people go in fear of the dentist's drill, especially those who are allergic to anaesthetics. It was good news for these when it was announced in 1953 that Dr Carl R. Oman of the Operative Division of the Columbia University Dental College and Dr Edmund Applebaum had successfully performed the first ultrasound tooth-drilling operation on patients. Compared with orthodox methods it was painless.

By ultrasound, tooth structure is removed by very light taps of minute abrasive particles at 20,000 to 30,000 taps a second and the total force needed to cut teeth is only a few ounces, against pounds when a metal drill is used. Unfortunately an entirely new method and technique is needed, which few dentists have time to master, so not many in practice have embraced it. Those now in dental school will doubtless be taught the new techniques.

But almost simultaneously with the invention of the ultrasound drill came the development of a new high-speed orthodox drill with cutting speeds of more than 100,000 rpm which needs only light pressure to operate it, and this, for the present at any rate, has superseded the ultrasonic drill.

ULTRASOUND AND HEAT

It has been claimed that ultrasound can relieve pain, stimulate, soothe and improve tissue nutrition, inhibit the sympathetic nervous system and dilate blood vessels. It is known that nerve tissue is more susceptible to ultrasound than any other tissue, and that ultrasound can block the nerve impulses along the nerve fibres, but it is doubtful whether this soothing effect is more than temporary.

Similar stimulating effects can be produced by the application of heat, for all energy entering the tissues is converted into heat. If, however, heat produced by ultrasound rises to a lethal level it may pass from bone to adjacent tissue, destroying it.

USES OF MICROWAVE RADIATION

In Australia ionizing radiation has been employed on an industrial scale for years in the destruction of anthrax bacilli from baled goat-hair used to make carpets, but doses are very low compared with those used for food. Considerable research has been done by the US Atomic Energy Commission to preserve fish, fruit and vegetables at the Low Temperature Research Station, Cambridge; the Atomic Energy Research Station, Wantage; and the Torrey Research Institute, Aberdeen, where gamma-radiation cobalt-60 is used to sterilize medical and surgical equipment.

The ion is simply an atom or part of a molecule with an electrical discharge. We inhale ions all the time, as they are present in the atmosphere, but they increase vastly during electrical storms. To produce ions artificially air is passed over a radioactive source or an ultraviolet lamp, and as the air particles move into range they acquire a charge which converts them into ions.

Why a Shower Refreshes More Than a Bath

E. T. Pierce and A. C. Wilson of the Stanford Research Institute studied the effects of water as it sprayed from a bathroom shower and found that a field of negative electrification was created. The same action takes place in a waterfall, in the air just after a thunderstorm, or when rain falls, especially after a long dry period. The air seems sweet, fresh and clean because it is charged with negative ions. In 1967 the Russian scientist Igor Ostryakov found during experiments that the right amount of negative ionization 'speeds up plant growth, suppresses the development of fungus micro-organisms, improves the blood-composition of tested animals, and retards the growth of tumours.' Inhaling high concentrations of negative ions also relieves hay fever and asthma.

The benefits of ionization extend far beyond the respiratory ailments. In Philadelphia doctors treated seventy-five patients suffering from burns with antibiotics and ascorbic acid, then exposed them for up to sixty minutes to ionized air. There was an immediate reduction of pain, the need for narcotics was substantially reduced, children stopped crying, and all pain vanished within a few hours.

Dr Walter H. Eddy, Professor of Physiological Chemistry at Columbia University, placed thirty mice with lung cancer in a cage with ordinary atmosphere, and another thirty into a cage charged with negative-ionized atmosphere. After two months twenty-two of the mice in the ordinary air died, and autopsies showed that in every case the lung changes were malignant. Only two in the other batch died, and subsequent autopsies showed no signs of the disease. Experiments are being carried on.

DISADVANTAGES OF RADIATION

The main disadvantage of irradiating food is that flavour and colour are often affected, there is a diminution of the sulphydryl groups in proteins, much destruction of glutamic acid and serin in frozen meat, and significant changes in other amino-acids. Vitamin content is also reduced: in milk 70 per cent of vitamin A, 40 per cent of carotinoids, 40 per cent of thiamin and 20 per cent of vitamin C. During experiments with rats it was found that those fed on irradiated. meat for some time suffered haemorrhages, but this may have been caused by the change in their eating habits. Heat from irradiation kills most types of bacteria, but no more probably than the heat from a kitchen stove.

TISSUE DAMAGE

Microwaves do not raise the temperature of the body in the

way that heat does. They seem to disregard the surface of the skin but burrow below, and the combined effect of heat and electric and magnetic forces causes tissue damage. P. A. Breysse states: 'Certain tissues in the human body are more vulnerable to damage because of poor heat conduction to surrounding tissues or lack of an adequate blood supply. The eyes, testes and some of the abdominal organs are more susceptible to damage from over-exposure to microwaves than other organs.'*

IS THERE DANGER IN MICROWAVE OVENS?

When it was established that microwaves could break down tissue, scientists applied them to flesh foods and found that their tissues could be broken down within minutes to produce meat that was tender and appetizing – and the microwave oven was born. Most hospitals in America and some in Britain installed them, for eggs could be cooked in thirty seconds, potatoes in five minutes and a roast in half an hour. The oven was hailed as a time and fuel saver and a boon to mankind. But, as in the case of every invention meant for the benefit of Man, it had disadvantages. Dr Alfred L. Frechette, Commissioner of the Massachusetts Department of Health, reported that of the seventy-four microwave ovens (some British) tested by his department, eighteen produced more than the safe radiation level, which is ten milliwatts per square centimetre. Where there is a leakage radiations can be responsible for the formation of cataracts in the eyes of those who bend over and peer through the glass doors to see whether food is cooked.

British standards are even more stringent. These state that: (1) microwave ovens must be properly sited so that they are

---

* *This Week in Public Health*, 19 January 1970 (Dept of Public Health, Massachusetts, WA).

away from seated workers, or where people at home may sit for long periods; (2) ovens should be regularly serviced and maintained; (3) servicing must include a check on the levels of microwave leakage, which is likely to increase with the age of the cooker through the distortion of the seals; and (4) a microwave cooker should not be used if the leakage level exceeds the recommended maximum – 5 milliwatts per square centimetre at 5 centimetres from any point on the outside of the cooker – until it has been repaired.

The ovens are boosted by manufacturers, and their salesmen rarely stress the dangers of leakage. Though food cooks far more rapidly many state that it does not retain its full flavour, and the surfaces of meats lack the appetizing brown colour which makes the mouth water, so most cooks brown them in conventional ovens, which means more cooking time and the further destruction of nutrients. It has also been established that microwaves do not destroy salmonella bacteria as effectively as traditional methods, and to ensure their destruction meats should be heated till mid-point temperatures reach at least 350 F.

Bearing these facts in mind, those who wish to instal microwave ovens should make sure they are guaranteed leakproof and that mid-point temperatures are adequate. The World Health Organization stated in 1966: 'Radiation could be a valuable means of preserving food but only if carefully controlled. The advantages are not a sufficient warrant for its indiscriminate use because repeated radiation, which kills some micro-organisms but not others, could lead to the development of an increasingly resistant strain.'

STRENGTHENING METAL

Ultrasonic waves have many uses in industry. When iron or steel is in the molten stage it contains pockets of gas which on cooling remain as air spaces and weaken the structure. When treated by ultrasonic waves the gas is pressed together into large bubbles which escape, leaving the steel free from weakening pockets.

There are innumerable ways of applying ultrasonics to industry, one being in photography. The emulsion for films which produced 'grain' in miniature photography was a serious problem when enlargements were made; by subjecting the emulsion to ultrasonic waves during manufacture, the emulsion is broken down into microscopic particles and the 'grain' effect is avoided.

DESTRUCTIVE FORMS OF VIBRATION

Vibrations can also drive humans and animals mad and, if continued for any length of time, destroy them. In 1971 the Gas Council installed a £3,000,000 compressor 600 yards from a pig farm at West Bilney, Norfolk, which created a roar like a jet fighter pulling out of a dive. The effect on the pigs was disastrous, causing them to run round in circles and hurl themselves against the wire that fenced them in. Five died and most of the others were so seriously affected that the farmer claimed damages from the Council.

BOOM TESTS

The American government has carried out a series of tests to discover the effects of sonic booms on houses and found that 'low level' booms seem to retard the deterioration and ageing of houses.

Mr J. M. Wiggins Jnr, a civil engineer who directed the government sponsored tests at White Sands, New Mexico for two years, wrote a paper in which he stated that when homes were subjected to repeated booms they had a lower rate of structural defects than boom-free homes. His theory is that the gentle shaking the structure receives from a boom relieves accumulated stress and enables the walls to settle firmly on their foundations.

THE EFFECTS OF DESTRUCTIVE VIBRATIONS

Vibrations of very high frequency either go right through solid objects or bounce off them, doing comparatively little harm, but vibrations below the level of hearing can create a pendulum action that may build up to a destructive level. Stand close to the siren of an ocean-going liner and you will realize what a devastating effect the blast has on the eardrums and, if continued for long, on the body.

Science-fiction writers who make free use of 'death rays' to destroy the enemies of their heroes little realize how deadly these can be, though not in the form they envisage. Death rays are projected not in the form of light, but as sound.

NIKOLA TESLA*

Perhaps the first to make the 'death ray' a practical reality was Nikola Tesla, a name almost unknown to the general public. His inventive powers far exceeded those of Edison, who was virtually uneducated and made his ideas work by putting them into practice and then finding out what was wrong. Tesla was a brilliant scientist and engineer, who worked out his ideas in his head; then, when they were complete, put them into practice. Invariably they worked! He is renowned chiefly for making alternating current a possibility when everyone – including Edison – said it was impracticable. First he offered his invention to Edison, who turned it down, and eventually to George Westinghouse, who paid him a million dollars for it. Alternating current generators were then installed in the great power station at Niagara Falls, and homes and factories hundreds of miles away were given light and energy. Direct current, Edison's invention, cannot be transmitted for more than a few hundred yards, as cables to transmit it further would be too thick, heavy and costly. Today the

* Tesla was born on the stroke of midnight between 9 and 10 July 1856 in Smiljan, now Yugoslavia. He died on 7 January 1943.

whole world uses Tesla's system. His ideas were so far ahead of his time that few could be induced to take them seriously. Among them were radio and television.

Tesla's Oscillator*

In 1896 Tesla made a mechanical oscillator on the upper floor of a building on the north side of Houston Street, New York, about 300 feet north of the Police Headquarters. When he set his machine in motion the oscillations so built up that heavy pieces of furniture vibrated, the windowpanes seemed to sing, the floor jumped up and down and the walls juddered. In the police HQ desks jigged and rattled, plaster fell from ceilings, windows splintered and water ran from burst pipes.

Tesla had created a minor earthquake, and the police, who knew all about his experiments, raced to his laboratory to try to stop him from wrecking the town. They got there in time to find him with a sledgehammer in his hands, smashing his oscillator, for it was not much use switching off the current as the oscillations would have continued at a slower pace for some time, doing untold damage.

He did not continue with experiments in oscillation, for having succeeded he lost interest and immersed himself in something else. He could have been the richest man in America had he concentrated in putting half his ideas into practical use, but money – except to further other ideas – had no appeal for him.

PROFESSOR VLADIMIR GAVREAU

In 1960 Professor Gavreau, head of the Electro-Acoustics and Automation Laboratories of the French National Scientific Research Centre outside Marseilles, almost resigned his job because he always felt ill while at work. Then suddenly he realized that nausea invariably attacked him only when he was in

* See John O'Neill, *The Life of Nikola Tesla* (Spearman, 1968).

his office at the top of the building. He tried, without success, to find the cause.

One day, quite by accident, he leant against a wall, felt the whole room vibrating at a very low frequency, and traced the cause to an air-conditioning plant on the roof of a nearby building. It then struck him that his office was just the right shape and distance to resonate in sympathy, and the rhythm – seven cycles a minute – made him sick. Had he not been an acoustics expert the cause might never have occurred to him.

Noise that Killed

As head of the department he decided to initiate experiments into infrasound, and he and his colleagues built a gigantic whistle which they connected to a compressed air hose and turned it on full. The effect on their bodies was shattering. Every organ started to vibrate: stomach, heart, lungs, liver, kidneys and spleen. The unfortunate man who turned on the blast fell dead on the spot, and a post-mortem revealed that all his internal organs had been mashed into a jelly by the vibration.

The whistle was switched off at once, but the entire team was sick for hours. Those in laboratories adjacent or nearby were also very sick, and extremely cross with Gavreau for subjecting them to such an ordeal.

This did not put a stop to his experiments, however, though he proceeded with much greater caution. He knew, of course, that high-intensity sounds could prove deadly, for R. Levavasseur, a colleague, had modified an ordinary police whistle by adding a resonant cavity at one end, which increased its power four hundred times. When blown, the effect on Levavasseur was frightening and he is now a chronic invalid.

A Modern Jericho

Among the test machines built in Gavreau's laboratory is a siren which emits a low-pitched note of 37 cycles a second (roughly the lowest 'E' on a piano). When operated it set the building vibrating like a giant pipe organ and cracked some of the walls. It was shut off at once, for had it continued the structure would have collapsed.

Another was a whistle which caused the nostrils of a colleague to vibrate so violently that he recovered a sense of smell he had lost three years previously, indicating that vibrations may have good as well as bad effects. Only experiment will show which.

Gavreau thinks that some of the infrasounds caused by heavy trucks, machinery, ventilating fans, etc. in big cities may be instrumental in producing many of the allergies from which millions suffer today, but did not in the past, and for which doctors seem to have no cure. This is a field in which the researcher must proceed with the utmost caution, for no one knows what will happen until suddenly and without warning disaster may overwhelm those taking part in the project.

German experiments have also proved that inaudible low frequencies can produce nausea, fright and panic; and in America powerful rockets which also produce low frequencies have caused blurred vision, dizziness, lassitude and disturbing vibration of the chest and stomach.

Experts at Southampton University are carrying out research at the Institute of Sound and Vibration, and Dr J. G. Guignard, head of the department, agrees with Gavreau in thinking that industrial vibration is the cause of much untraced illness.

SOUND AS A WEAPON OF WAR

Inevitably governments throughout the world turn their energies to harnessing new inventions that will bring victory in time of war, but so far no machines for producing vibrations that will kill have been of practical value. Those that are lethal have an extremely limited range and are probably a greater danger to their operators than to the enemy. If longer ranges are desired the vibration-generators would be far too bulky and lack mobility and could not compete with weapons already in use. The safety factor is all-important but there is little doubt that in time this problem will be overcome – as such problems are – and instead of blasting people to their deaths it will be possible to pulp the organs of opponents into an amorphous mass. This will bring accompanying benefits: there will be no wounded to care for; no doctors and nurses will be needed; and hospitals will be superfluous. Death will be instantaneous – and, one assumes, painless.

3

Electricity is
the Basis of Life

In 1637 Descartes, a man of many parts, established the theory of reflex action and demonstrated that certain actions are involuntary and incoercible, depending on the activity of the nervous centres, and more especially the brain. They are set in motion by a stimulation of the senses, and by a simple mechanism 'animal spirits' travel along the nerves, causing muscular contractions.

In 1670, in the course of experiments, Jan Swammerdam, a Dutch apothecary, discovered that when the sciatic nerve is mechanically stimulated, cut or pinched, the gastrocnemius muscle contracts. In the eighteenth century another experiment demonstrated that when the electricity accumulated in a Leyden jar, or produced by an electrical machine, was applied to any portion of the human frame it induced muscle contraction.

Then at the end of the eighteenth century a revolutionary discovery was made by Luigi Galvani, Professor of Anatomy and Gynaecology in Bologna, and Alessandro Volta, a physicist. Galvani said that electricity is produced in the muscles, Volta that it is the product of two metals. To prove his theory Volta invented the electric battery – and electro-physiology was born.

Not till the middle of the nineteenth century was much further progress made in this new science. Then better technical resources were discovered by the Italian Matteucci and the German Du Bois-Reymond, both physiologists. Soon followed the discovery by Magendie in France and Bell in England that sensation and motor power have separate channels of conduction. Slowly brick after brick was added to the edifice of knowledge by men like Paul Broca and Wernicke, and in 1870 Fritsch and Hitzig proved that certain regions of the cerebral cortex are susceptible to stimulation and that the application of alternating current to the precentral convolution of the brain gives rise to contractions limited to certain groups of muscles. If the current is strong enough it will produce an epileptic attack.

INTERNAL ELECTRICITY

All this led to the belief that the nervous impulses travelling along the nerves to various parts of the body were ordinary electric currents, but as electricity travels at 186,326 miles per second this was obviously not so, for the impulses measured along the sciatic nerve of a frog travel at only 30 metres a second.

Throughout Europe and America research continued apace by men now famous in the field of physiology: Golgi, Ramon y Cajal, Waller, Nissal, Morat, Sherrington, Lapicue, Lipmann, Erlander, Gasser, Pavlov, Magnus, the Weber brothers, Adrian, and later by scientists in Asia and South America. E. N. Goodman found that the electrical potential of the stomach varies when full and empty, and Dr Richter of Johns Hopkins Hospital, Baltimore, developed a recording machine to render diagnosis more accurate than before.

BRAGG AND HALDANE

Sir William Bragg said: 'Electricity is the way matter behaves,' and in 1924 Warburg discovered that the oxygen we breathe unites with an enzyme which is mainly protein. Then J. B. S. Haldane found by experiment that the same process takes place in green plants, moths and rats! The process takes place in all living creatures.

The chemicals which comprise the body – carbon, iron, nitrogen, oxygen, calcium, phosphorus, silicon, etc – combine to form a perfect electric battery, and the food we eat and the liquid we drink enables the body to recharge itself. How exactly, we don't know. Only at death does this process stop, for death is caused by the disintegration of the 'plates' of the human body due to faulty feeding and wrong living, or merely because the organs have worn out.

If one constantly eats the wrong foods, imbibes too much strong liquor, breathes tainted air, thinks the wrong thoughts and lives riotously, the body will degenerate more rapidly than is normal or natural, though there are some bodies which, through heredity or causes we do not understand, resist this degenerative process to a remarkable degree.

WE DIE WHEN THE BRAIN DIES

If Man did not have a brain he would probably be able to exist indefinitely, for Dr Alexis Carrel said: 'It is only because the cells are subject to a mysterious energy released by the brain that they die.' Incidentally, tissue cells can replace themselves, but once a nerve cell dies it cannot be replaced.

Man is not unique in being able to produce body electricity. Fireflies do so, and so do some species of fish. Dr H. S. Burr and F. S. C. Northopp of Yale, who conducted thousands of experiments mainly with eggs, found electrical fields in most elementary kinds of embryo. Electricity is a form of matter, and all matter consists of vibrations.

BREATHING IS CONTROLLED ELECTRICITY

Breathing, a function we perform involuntarily, is an extremely complicated operation and is controlled in the medulla oblongata, a part of the brain. From one group in the medulla rhythmic impulses run down the spinal cord to the phrenic nerve which controls the diaphragm, and to the intercostal muscles.

The heart is also controlled by electrical impulses. While heading a group of scientists at the Los Angeles County Heart Association's cardiovascular research laboratories in the UCLA Medical Centre in February 1964, Dr Alan J. Brady discovered that 'at every heartbeat a tiny area of specialized human tissue, located in the wall of the right side of the heart, sent out an electrical impulse.' This set off a train of events which released energy locked in ATP (adenosine triphosphate), the muscle fuel. It is this interaction which makes the muscle fibres contract, though it is not quite clear how the proteins act.

Muscle Cells

Dr Brady's theory is that muscle cells are like miniature electric batteries. When the muscle is relaxed the cells have a negative charge on the inside of the membrane (cell envelope) and a positive charge on the outside. These charges are produced by electrically charged atoms or ions of sodium and potassium; and in a cell at rest the potassium ions predominate inside, and the sodium ions outside.

When a spark from the heart reaches the cell it acts like a switch and reverses the charge by causing the sodium ions to rush out. Experiments have shown that this switching action releases calcium (we don't yet know how), which is present normally in the cell, into the cell sites where the contractile proteins are stored. Tests have proved that calcium must be present for this to happen; the more calcium the greater the contraction. Calcium seems to be the medium that puts the contractile machinery into action.

To all with a knowledge of the chemistry of the body it will be clear that a certain amount of carbon dioxide must be carried in the blood in the form of sodium bicarbonate, for without it there would be no sodium ions and no cell for the spark from the heart to activate. Nature works in a mysterious way, but as our knowledge increases her ways become clearer.

ELECTRICAL THEORY IS NOT NEW

The theory that all body tissues are electrically negative except those of the brain and the nervous system, which are electrically positive because they take up oxygen at more rapid rate, was first expounded by the American surgeon Dr George W. Crile of Cleveland at a meeting of the American Association for the Advancement of Science in 1940. He said that the processes of the body are based on a definite series of radiations of various wavelengths, from ultraviolet to infrared, which emanate from living substances in the body, and the activity of these 'life rays' is increased by processes such as malignant disease or narcotics.

Much of this must also have been known to the yogis 6000 years ago, for in one branch of yoga known as Kriya, breathing exercises are practised to recharge the blood vessels with oxygen, which is supposed to be transmitted to the brain and the spinal centres. This is done to retard ageing, revitalize the tissues and charge the blood with energy. The technique is very different from ordinary deep breathing, and few in Britain or America have a sound knowledge of Kriya yoga.

BODY ELECTRICITY

The electricty in our bodies is self-generated and starts with our first breath – perhaps even in the womb – and the power is cut off at death. It is different and of a subtler nature than the current produced by a generator, which can be stored in batteries and tapped when needed, and which can be stepped up and down by transformer and transported hundreds of miles.

Body electricity produces vibrations which affect every person and every object with whom one comes into contact. Each one of us is affected by vibrations emanating from other persons and objects, even from bodies millions of miles away, such as the sun, moon and the planets.

The vibrations exuding from some people are so powerful that they have merely to place their hands on the sick and suffering to cure disease or alleviate pain. Dr T. Gerald Garry said: 'I knew an Austrian masseuse whose work formed a striking example of the "life-ray" theory. She advertised "electrical massage" but the massage had nothing to do with electricity as we understand it. It appeared to be under her personal control. Before the electric force or whatever it was became active, she closed her eyes and was apparently in deep concentration. Then some slight muscular tremors were perceptible, after which the battery was in complete working order. Her fingers would attract little bits of paper and other light objects as if they were a powerful magnet. She was usually somewhat exhausted after an exhibition of this kind, but the potential strength of the radiations had never diminished since her youth. At the time when I knew her she was about fifty-five. She seemed to live in a universe of ethereal and invisible waves endowed with great energy.'[*]

When such healers work for long periods the current from their bodies is discharged from them into their patients, leaving them exhausted. That is why they should not work for many hours at a stretch, and under no circumstances should they push themselves, otherwise they too will succumb to disease. To retain their powers healers need regular rest each day and periods of recuperation; and good simple food and drink. They should also live moral lives and think creatively, otherwise they may lose their powers.

ETHEL DE LOACH

That the radiation which streams from a healer's body varies in strength during rest and healing periods was demonstrated

* Dr T. Gerald Garry, *African Doctor* (Gifford, 1939).

in photographs taken of Ethel de Loach of New Jersey, by Douglas Dean. When at rest Kirlian* photographs showed that only a dark blue radiation flowed out of her finger tips, but when she was healing a long orange and red flare, in addition to the dark blue, was seen at a point below the tips. The glow during healing was far more intense than either before or after.

THE AURA

For centuries the yogis have known that the human aura reflected the personality of the person who wore it, for the aura is an emanation of one of the seven principles of Man. (These are: (1) The Physical Body; (2) The Astral Body; (3) Prana or the Vital Force; (4) The Instinctive Mind; (5) The Intellect; (6) The Spiritual Mind; (7) The Spirit.) The aura radiates energy which is visible to sensitives but not to others. Sensitives have a highly developed consciousness and have always been able to see the halos which adorned the heads of saints and outlined their bodies. They were, of course, scoffed at and ridiculed by the more earthy types who could not see this manifestation. Some auras can be seen by people with a comparatively undeveloped grade of psychic power, but only the most developed psychics can see auras of the sixth and seventh principles.

Paintings of Christ usually show an aura surrounding his body, and the New Testament says: 'And He was transfigured before them; and his face did shine as the sun, and his raiment was as white as the light.' (Matthew 17.2.)

ETHER

The yogis say that ether formed the four higher or finer sub-

* See page 81.

planes of the physical body, the sub-planes being: (1) First Etheric or Atomic; (2) Second Etheric or Sub-Atomic; (3) Third Etheric or Super-Etheric; (4) Fourth Etheric or Etheric; and collectively they are known as the Etheric Plane.

The Etheric Double is the counterpart of the Dense Physical Body, pervading and sustaining it, formed of the matter of the four sub-planes. It serves as the vehicle of life (*prana*), passing on the same to the denser matter that we perceive with the normal physical senses.

The aura is the manifestation of the higher substance that extends beyond the physical body, and trained psychics (clairvoyants) can usually distinguish five auras, of which the aura of health appears to be the lowest and most dense. All this was dismissed as superstitious poppycock by scientists in the nineteenth century, and indeed until comparatively recently.

An aura clothes one like a fine invisible overcoat, and every aura has a distinctive odour. It is this, for instance, that a bloodhound smells when it is given an article of clothing belonging to a missing person or a criminal. Leon F. Whitney, whose bloodhounds were famous in America for their trailing powers forty years ago, said that from time to time his wonderful sleuths would raise their muzzles into the air and sniff the aura of the person they were tracking. Even when criminals waded into rivers and walked upstream their auras persisted and his hounds followed them successfully.

MESMER

Franciscus Antonius Mesmer (1733–1815) was perhaps the first of the moderns to realize that every human being is affected by radiations. His graduation thesis at the Medical School of the University of Vienna was on the influence of the planets on Man, for at that time most scientists and physicians believed in, or practised, astrology. By passing his hands over the sick, or by touching them, he caused a 'fluence' of animal magnetism to flow into their bodies, curing or relieving them of pain.

Not long after, Goethe advanced the theory that the Universe was not the lifeless body that Newton had imagined but was filled with life and colour, and he suggested that vibrations emanating from the human body should be made the subject of serious study.

Mesmer had a considerable following, though many of his theories were discredited because he could not prove them to the satisfaction of scientists. Nor was Goethe taken seriously, for his reputation had been won in the fields of philosophy and poetry.

REICHENBACH

Another to try to impose his unorthodox ideas on the scientific world was Baron Karl von Reichenbach (1788–1869), an industrial chemist renowned for his discovery of creosote and other chemical compounds. He was among the first to carry out experiments with psychics and found that they could feel a current of cold air at the north pole of a magnet and distinguish a bluish flame of vapour in the dark.

He also found that inanimate objects such as stones, rocks and gems produced similar phenomena, and he called the radiations emanating from these Odic Force. His *Researches on Magnetism, Electricity, Light, Crystallization and Chemical Attraction in Their Relation to Vital Forces*, published in 1850, describes his work.

It was this force that William Reich called Orgone energy. Later Dr Bircher-Benner said it was electric energy and suggested it was a component of sunlight. Others have called it ether, bio-cosmic energy, cosmic orgone energy, and the yogis call it *prana*. The nineteenth century was the age of scientific materialism, and inevitably Reichenbach was labelled a crank.

REICH

Wilhelm Reich (1897–1957), author of thirty books and an

early collaborator of Sigmund Freud, was a brilliant scientist and psychoanalyst who claimed to have discovered a new kind of energy akin to static electricity, which he called orgone. This, he said, was bluish in colour, emanated from the sun, and affected all living creatures. Clouds and water accumulate orgone, which is the best guarantor of health. Reich made blankets consisting of layers of organic and inorganic material in which orgone was trapped. These, he claimed, prevented colds, rheumatism, arthritis and even polio. More than eighty patients treated by him were restored to health; but as his methods did not conform to orthodox teachings the American Medical Association denounced him as a charlatan and, when he refused to curb his activities, prosecuted him. Reich believed that orgone is stored in the body and is visible to psychics.

We now know that these body radiations are not generated in the same way as the current that flows through cables into electric lights, cooking stoves, TV and radio sets and other appliances used in the home. They are so minute that they are not measured in volts, amperes and watts, and their intensity can be measured only by instruments specially designed.

WALTER KILNER

It must have taken courage for Dr Walter Kilner of St Thomas's Hospital, London, to delve into the nature of the human aura and declare that he had seen it, for those who had done so were called 'deluded folk' and said to be mentally unbalanced. St Thomas's has always been a progressive institution, for the first demonstration of Roentgen Rays took place there in 1896. Kilner, head of the department of electrotherapy, heard that Professor Blondlot of Nancy University had announced the discovery of a new form of radiation which he called N-rays. These emanated from the human body and from many other substances.

Kilner constructed a screen and in 1911 started a series of experiments during which he produced photographs of the aura of a perfectly shaped woman aged twenty-three enveloped in rays of bluish-grey light. Not till May 1921 did he write an article for *Science and Invention Magazine*, in which he described his apparatus, known as a dicyanin screen, which consisted of two glass plates one eighth of an inch apart, the space between them being filled with an alcoholic solution of dicyanin, through which the human aura was clearly visible.

He confirmed the claim that auric emanations are divided into three parts: the outer aura, inner aura and the etheric double, which consists of a narrow band or void from one sixteenth of an inch to an eighth of an inch from the body. Adjacent is the inner aura extending about five inches; the outer aura, ovoid in shape, widest at the hips and tapering towards the legs. On average it extends about eight inches from the inner aura.

Eventually as a result of his findings he wrote *The Human Atmosphere*, published in 1921,* and no other work on the subject seems to have appeared till 1937, when Oscar Bagnall produced *The Origin and Properties of The Human Aura.** Bagnall used pinacynol and methalen blue in his screen instead of dicyanin.

Kilner's were not merely academic experiments. He was convinced that the aura indicated the state of health and was the result of nutrition, exercise (including breathing) and control of thought processes. He observed that fatigue, disease, excessive cold or heat and changes of mood altered the size and colour of the aura, and he gave case histories in his book. 'I am certain,' he wrote, 'that a photographic picture of the size, shape and condition of the human aura is not only possible but will shortly be made, enabling the aura to become of still greater assistance in medical diagnosis.'

SEMYON AND VALENTINA KIRLIAN

After the 1939–45 war in which 20,000 Russian towns and

* Both published by Kegan Paul.

villages were devastated by the Nazis, Kirlian, an electrician and amateur photographer, and his wife, were making adjustments to equipment they had designed in 1938 when a high-voltage wire sparked across a film, resulting in a photograph. It was a pure accident, for neither lens nor camera had been used, but the film recorded a strange luminescence, invisible to the human eye, which seemed to be emitted by all living objects.

This technique had been first discovered by Nikola Tesla, inventor of the high-frequency resonant transmitter or Tesla Coil, but as with so many of his discoveries, Tesla went no further with this one, which at the time seemed to have no practical value.

Among those who heard of the Kirlians' experiments, however, was a biologist who asked them to make 'energy pictures or flares' from two identical leaves. When developed one showed a bright luminescence, but the other was extremely dull. The Kirlians were disappointed, but not so the biologist, who was jubilant. 'This leaf' – he pointed to the luminescent picture – 'is from a healthy plant; the other from a diseased plant.' The luminescence or aura of the leaves indicated their state of health, just as it had in Kilner's screen.

The Kirlians then photographed a multitude of objects by the same process, including coins and other inanimate objects, but it was not for another ten years that anyone in a position of authority took much notice of them. Then in the early 1960s the USSR Ministry of Health realized that their discovery might be of value in medical diagnosis and awarded them a research grant, but Dr Lev Federov, who recommended it, died, and the bureaucrats in the Ministry cut off their supply. Eventually, twenty-five years after their discovery, a conference of scientists was held in Alma Ata and papers on the Kirlians' and similar work dealing with 'biological energy' were read.

These aroused interest not only in the USSR but in America, and Professor Thelma Moss, head of the Neuro-psychiatric Institute of the University of California, wrote to Russia and received an invitation to visit Alma Ata, where Professor Vladimir Inyushin had taken up the Kirlians' work and progressed a stage further. He said that the luminescence in the Kirlian pictures had been caused not by an electrical state of the organism but by 'a biological plasma body' which is only another name for aura, etheric, or astral body. It was found later that this luminescence is concentrated in more than seven hundred points in the human body, which correspond to the acupuncture points in the old Chinese system of healing.

LIVING ORGANISMS CREATE AN ELECTRIC FIELD

Some years ago, while studying 'bee language', scientists in Ryazan, Central Russia, found that a weak electrical field is formed round flying bees and proved that this field, whose tension varied, played some role in the communication between insects. They then devised a portable electronic apparatus capable of recording the smallest oscillation of sounds created by the bees and set up a tiny microphone in the roof of the hive to determine the nature of the sounds and their variation. By this means they managed to control the physiological processes taking place in the bee family, and they hope eventually that it will be possible to increase the flow of honey and reduce the amount of work the bees perform.

In 1967 in a public demonstration at a meeting of the Leningrad Society of Natural Sciences, Professor Pavel Gulyayev, head of the laboratory of physiological cybernetics at the University, registered and measured the electrical field of a nerve on an electro-auragram. The instrument recorded an electrical field around the nerve of a frog at a distance of 25 centimetres, and a human heart at a distance of 10 centimetres. This confirmed experimentally the hypothesis of the existence of electrical field around an active nerve, muscle, heart and brain. It proved also that the human body has an electrical field surrounding it, which can be recorded on a highly sensitive probe amplifier.

'Electro-auragramming changes radically our views on living organism,' said Professor Gulyayev, 'shedding light on the mechanism of biological relationships between them, relationships which were impossible to prove materially before.' He believes that it will be possible to register the brain's electrical field, though so far this had not been achieved.

DR ALBERT ABRAMS

Dr Albert Abrams of San Francisco inherited a considerable fortune, and after qualifying as a doctor he studied advanced medicine in Heidelberg, where his interest in the healing power of vibrations was stimulated by Professor de Sauer, who was engaged in research on mitogenic radiation. On his return to America Abrams lectured on pathology and was appointed head of Stanford University Medical School. He mastered the art of percussion, and by tapping the body to produce resonating sounds he found clues to disease.

One day he switched on an X-ray apparatus which muffled the resonant note he received while tapping a patient and realized that the dulling occurred only when the patient faced east and west, indicating that there was a connection between the geomagnetic field and the vibrations. Later he found that a similar effect was produced by a man with a cancerous ulcer on one lip, even though the X-ray machine was not working.

After scores of experiments with patients suffering from various diseases he was convinced that the nerve fibres in the epigastric region respond to the stimulus of X-rays. This step led to others and eventually he designed a machine called an 'oscilloclast', which he used for diagnosing and curing disease.

In 1919 he set out to teach other physicians how to use his machine, and in 1922 stated in the *Physio-Clinical Journal* that by using his machine he could diagnose disease in the bodies of patients thousands of miles from his surgery. Eventually this led to the development of the Abrams Box, which was further refined and improved by Dr Ruth Drown in America and George de la Warr in Britain. Abrams died in 1922.

Though these developments did not have the seal of approval of the American Medical Association, Abrams had much too high a reputation for them to denounce and persecute him.

DR RUTH DROWN

Dr Ruth Drown, a chiropractor in Los Angeles and one of Abrams' disciples, was less fortunate. She improved the Abrams Box and developed a camera to photograph the organs and tissues of patients, using only a drop of their blood. This she also accomplished though some of them were hundreds of miles away; what is more, her camera took photographs in cross section, which cannot be done by X-rays.

Though this pioneer in the new science of radionics was granted a patent in Britain for her apparatus her claim was disallowed by the FDA in America, who said that it originated in the realms of science fiction. Her equipment was confiscated and the authorities got into touch with *Life* magazine, which printed an article branding her as a charlatan. This so disheartened Ruth Drown that she died of grief, but not before she left behind a record of her work in *Theory and Techniques of Radio Therapy*, the first major account in English on the subject.

Dr G. W. Wigglesworth and his brother, an electronics engineer, took up where she left off and developed an apparatus which they called a 'pathoclast' or disease-breaker. They then founded the Pathometric Association and their research was continued and advanced by T. Galen Hieronymus of Kansas City.

MAGNETISM

Every student of electrical engineering knows that if a sheet of paper is placed over a magnet and iron filings are sprinkled on it, they will invariably arrange themselves in regular curves, each curve being linked to the poles of the magnet in such a way that it can be regarded as entering at one point and leaving it at another. Petrus Periegrinus observed this phenomenon in the thirteenth century and tried to find a reason for the strange behaviour of the filings. His experiments were recorded in a scientific journal in 1717. It was these that suggested to Faraday his conception of 'lines of force' and in return led to the theory of conduction – that is, if a circuit is moved about in the neighbourhood of another circuit carrying an electric current, a current will be induced in the moving circuit. Oersted proved later that every electric current is surrounded by lines of magnetic force.

On a sphere containing a charge of electricity the lines of force emerge radially in all directions and the presence of another body will cause the lines which would normally pass over it to bend to its shape. After numerous and complicated experiments Oersted concluded that these 'lines of force' were similar to light waves and had about the same velocity of light. However, only after much further research, by Maxwell in 1875, J. J. Thomson in 1881, Poynting in 1884, Hertz in 1886, and then by Lodge and Howard, was it discovered that if electric radiation was passed through large lenses it could be concentrated as light.

These exciting developments turned the footsteps of scientists towards the practical uses of electricity; to generators, motors, transformers, and to their use in industry. It was left to pathologists to investigate the behaviour of electricity in Man, in whose body the charges are infinitesimally smaller and travel far more slowly than the currents generated by iron magnets surrounded by many yards of copper wire. In Man the conductors are the nerves and the 'lines of force' are called 'force fields' by practitioners of radionics.

VICTOR TUSHLYAKOV

It was once thought that only iron and steel could be attracted or repelled by magnetic fields, but in 1967 Professor Victor Tushlyakov of the Leningrad Academy of Military Medical Sciences ran water through a magnetic field then used it to make soup and tea, and stewed fruit in it. When these were given to patients in a urological hospital in the city they were astonished to find that the 'magnetized water' which when analysed was no different to ordinary water had some mysterious property which dissolved kidney stones and prevented new ones from forming.

At the start of the experiment one fifth of each patient's normal intake of liquids was processed in a magnetic field, and this was gradually increased to 70 per cent. This opens up a new field in medicine and may have a much wider application, for no one knows how other liquids will act when 'magnetized'.

SIR JAGDIS CHANDRA BOSE

Like Reichenbach, Reich, Abrams, Drown and de la Warr, Jagdis Bose, as he is known in India, was so much in advance of his time that the *Encyclopedia Britannica* says that much of his work has not yet been properly evaluated.

When I was a boy in Calcutta, and later a student of electrical and mechanical engineering, Bose was revered by Bengalis and placed on a pedestal alongside Rabindranath Tagore. He was a physicist, physiologist and psychologist, and found out more about plant behaviour than anyone before or since. He was educated at St Xavier's College, a Christian Brothers' institution, where he was strongly influenced by Father Lafont, a Jesuit with an international reputation in astronomy. From there he moved to Christ's College, Cambridge, and on his return to India he was appointed Professor of Physics at Presidency College, Calcutta, then the premier college in the country.

Of such low repute were Indians held in the days of the Raj, however, that the Director of Public Instruction in Bengal held that no Indian was qualified to teach science and violently opposed his appointment. When Bose was appointed he decreed that his salary should be only half that paid to a British professor. Bose thereupon refused for three years to accept a penny of his salary, but during that period so brilliantly did he expound that his lectures were always crowded and the authorities were compelled, reluctantly, to recognize his genius, and awarded him full pay, with arrears. Even then he was not given a grant for research and his only assistant was an illiterate tinsmith.

Despite this handicap Bose managed to construct an apparatus to transmit Hertzian waves through the air, and in 1895 he proved to an audience presided over by Sir Alexander Mackenzie, Governor of Bengal, that electric waves could be sent from the lecture hall, through three intervening walls, to a room 75 feet away where they tripped a relay which threw a heavy iron ball, fired a pistol and exploded a small mine. This was a full year before Marconi, yet Marconi's claim as the first to transmit radio waves was recognized the following year.

Though Lord Lister, President of the British Association, and other scientists recommended to the government that an immediate grant of £49,000 should be awarded to establish a research centre at Presidency College, the Bengal Education Department, headed by influential members of the European Community, blocked the project.

METALS AND PLANTS HAVE FEELING

His lectures and other duties and the obstacles which blocked his path did not prevent Bose from undertaking original lines of research, details of which appeared in *Nature* in 1898. He maintained that metals are not inanimate objects and demonstrated that they were sensitive and responded in animal-like ways, showing a remarkable resemblance to muscles in the way they reacted, and recovering from fatigue after exertion if massaged or treated with warm water. He also showed that metals reacted to poisons in much the same way as muscular tissue.

Further research proved that plants, flowers and vegetables responded similarly. Bose used chloroform to anaesthetize a large pine tree and then had it uprooted and transplanted without the tree suffering a fatal shock, as often happens during such operations. In May 1901, at the invitation of Sir Michael Foster, he lectured and demonstrated his findings at the Royal Institution, where he was praised by Sir William Crookes, discoverer of thallium and radiant matter and inventor of the radiometer and spinthariscope, and by Sir Robert Austen, one of the world's leading authorities on metals.

At each step in his work Bose had to invent and design instruments to measure his findings, as none existed. In 1917 after he was officially recognized and knighted, his Institute for Research was established in Calcutta. He then invented an instrument called a crescograph with a 10,000-fold magnification to record the growth and changes in plants in as brief a period as one minute. He also found that growth could be either retarded or stimulated, depending on the way one handled them. His crescograph also showed, in less than fifteen minutes, the probable action of fertilizers, foods and stimulants.

THE JAPANESE CATFISH

We now know that some animals and plants are so sensitive that they can feel vibrations imperceptible to humans. There are innumerable instances of cats, dogs, rats and snakes fleeing from areas which were devastated by earthquakes or volcanoes soon after they left. In Japan, for instance, there are on average 1.6 earthquakes every twenty-four hours, not all, fortunately, catastrophic. But no matter how feeble the tremors the Japanese catfish (*Parasilarus Asotus*) responds to them. The fish are three feet long, ugly and whiskered, which gives them their name, and specimens are kept in large tanks and closely observed. Every few hours the tanks are tapped with a mallet. If an earthquake is imminent the fish grow agitated, swim to the surface, try to leap out of the water and swim round and round, after which they sink to the bottom. By observing them the authorities are warned of more than 80 per cent of earthquakes, for only the feeblest of tremors fail to agitate the fish.

THE WEATHER PLANT

Trees and plants are far more sensitive than most people imagine and are extremely susceptible to the vibrations caused by climatic changes. We know that the fir cone opens in dry weather and closes when it is going to rain. Professor J. F. Nowack discovered at the turn of the century that *Abrus precatorius nobilis*, a tropical plant, can foretell dry and wet weather, thunder in the offing, storms, fogs, changes of wind, a fall or rise in the barometer, and earthquakes! By observing its movements he foretold the calamitous earthquakes in Japan in 1892 and those that destroyed Martinique, San Francisco and parts of Jamaica. During the Vienna Exhibition in 1888 he exhibited a number of his plants, in which King Edward VII, then Prince of Wales, showed keen interest. The Professor predicted the very hour of a violent thunderstorm which wrecked a garden party given by the Prince, who on the strength of his forecast invited him to England, where he set up greenhouses in Denmark Hill, London.

In 1892 Nowack told the King of Italy that between June and August the following year Sicily would be visited by violent quakes after simultaneous eruptions of Etna and Vesuvius — events which came to pass. He also informed the Turkish Embassy in Vienna on 14 June 1894 that Constantinople would suffer an earthquake on the following day, and that there would be one in Adrianople in 1895, another in Salonika in 1902, and a third in Constantinople in 1905. It all came to pass as he had stated. In 1889 Nowack forecast a fire-damp explosion in Staffordshire in which 70 lives were lost.

By observing *Abrus* he predicted the storms which resulted in the loss of the North German Lloyd steamer *Sailier* on 8 December 1895 off Cape Corumbeta, when 281, including the pilot, went down; on 16 June 1896 he predicted the loss of the *Drummond Castle* off Ushant, with 240 lives; and on 23 July the same year, the loss of the German gunboat *Iltis* off the China coast. 'These disasters,' said Nowack, 'were not caused by strong currents or drifts but by deflections of the compass due to atmospheric and seismic disturbances.'

THE FATE OF THE ORIGINAL THINKER

The original thinker is rarely popular because he is an icono-clast and tends to shatter preconceived ideas and opinions. The moment he comes up with an idea or proposition which veers from the orthodox those entrenched in office feel threat-ened and their reputations at stake, so they close ranks. 'It can't be done,' they protest, 'or someone would have thought of it before,' and a dozen cogent reasons are advanced against it. One finds this attitude in every branch of science, but per-haps to a greater degree in medicine than elsewhere.

Whittle, inventor of jet propulsion, and Cockerell, pioneer of the hovercraft, were obstructed at every step. When Laith-waite thought of a new method of propulsion which will revo-lutionize travel and earn countless millions for Britain, he was denied one and a quarter million pounds for further research by the government, which fritters away hundreds of millions on worthless projects.

This attitude is an age-old one. M. G. Farmer of Boscawen, New Hampshire, USA, invented the incandescent lamp twenty years before Edison, but could find no one to take him seri-ously enough to put up the money for him to start. When Edison produced electric light Henry Morton, a famous re-search worker, said: 'Everyone acquainted with the subject of

electricity will recognize Edison's experiments as failures.'
When Graham Bell invented the telephone the authorities
bound him with so much red tape that they almost ensured the
failure of his device. Later one Astronomer-Royal stated:
'Space flight is utter bilge,' and Bishop Milton Wright, when
told that men might fly, pontificated: 'Flight is reserved for
the birds and you have been guilty of blasphemy!' He had sons
named Orville and Wilbur.

Not long ago Professor Henry Thring, head of the mechanical engineering department of Queen Mary's College,
London, tried to interest the National Coal Board in a
mechanical cutter which would solve our energy problems
within ten years, but though it had been shown to Lord Robens
and Sir Derek Ezra, both of whom were impressed, red tape
strangled his invention. This despite the fact that it would
guarantee 250,000,000 tons of coal for at least two hundred
years!

GEORGE DE LA WARR *

George de la Warr, Chief Engineering Assistant to an oil
refinery, Chief Constructional and Development Engineer of
the Firestone Rubber Company, and holder of important
government posts, became interested in medicine and radiations because he believed that Nature held the remedy for
most human and animal ailments, and that remedies could be
applied by the judicious use of plants and minerals. Why, he
asked, did medicine not make use of the radiations in Nature?

When one day a friend remarked casually that probably
each plant emitted its own musical note, his thoughts were
turned in a new direction. If the note was ultrasonic it would
be inaudible, but it might be in harmony with other kinds of
radiation. He first tried to pick up radiations on a crystal set,

* Langston Day, in collaboration with George de la Warr, *Matter in The Making* (Vincent Stuart, 1966).

but could get no response; then he tried a pendulum, and after that a water diviner's twig. All these experiments resulted in failure, to which was added the annoyance that his wife turned out to be a better water diviner than he!

Like all pioneers he was pig-headed enough to persist. He reasoned that if everything in Nature consisted of cells and each was a complete galvanic battery, then the sum total of their output should amount to a potential that could be measured. Using a sensitive spot galvanometer he carried out a number of experiments and found that the electrical potential of any plant was affected when it was treated with sound waves or when he and his wife, also a scientist, held it in their hands. He experimented with six potted plants, using variable resonators to produce the necessary sound waves, and discovered that every species of plant had its own special electrical conditions and would therefore need a corresponding mixture of sound waves to stimulate its growth. By trial and error and by countless experiments he designed a resonator to detect disease radiations. Unknown to him others had developed similar apparatus for the diagnosis and treatment of disease: Arthur Whiting of Victoria, Vancouver, Dr Albert Abrams, Dr Ruth Drown, Dr Boyd of Glasgow, Dr Guyon Richards, J. C. Maby, Starr White, and Dr G. W. Wigglesworth. De La Warr followed his own line of research, however, and worked out new tables of rates.

He realized that the diagnosis and treatment of disease can be carried out by physical irradiation or by distant radiation, but made it clear that radionic diagnosis is not a diagnosis of the physical body and should not be interpreted in the physical sense. Success depends to a certain extent on the operator. Mrs de la Warr found, for instance, that when using the diagnostic instrument *she* contributed something towards the general picture. By focusing her mind on the diseased organ she was able to produce resonance with the 'field force' of the organ of the patient under treatment. In the hands of capable practitioners the instrument worked efficiently but in the hands of others it was less effective.

Some of the Results

The de la Warrs began their original research into energy fields in 1942 and eventually developed the radionic camera, which can photograph projected thought! They also designed other instruments embodying sonic vibration, magnetics and colour for physical treatment. Some of their discoveries bordered on the fantastic. The suspected pregnancy of a woman in Ireland was photographed from Oxford, where they had their laboratories, and revealed the formation of a foetus.

When a crystalline substance was placed in the camera an image was produced which showed directional rays emanating from a common centre which could be identified with the rays of its constituted atoms. When the camera was tuned in to certain stages of the growth of a plant or a disease the patterns of subsequent growth could be controlled by the field force around the seed so that it could photograph leaves and flowers that were due to appear. When aconite flowers, for instance, were macerated and diluted as in homeopathy, the camera produced photos of the flowers. It seemed to be looking into the future.

The Prospecting Camera

One development was a prospecting camera which from Oxford located a subterranean water supply in the Middle East and, at the invitation of the Indian government, a pocket of natural gas in the foothills of the Himalayas. Not only humans and plants reacted to treatment but cows, horses, dogs and cats. When potted plants in Rhodesia were photographed by a Leica camera and the pictures submitted for treatment, this was carried out successfully from Oxford.

Opposition and Obstruction

A number of physicians, veterinary surgeons and scientists were persuaded to visit the laboratories and see what the instruments were capable of doing, but when the visitors failed to understand how the various apparatuses worked they condemned everything the de la Warrs were doing. Sometimes when important visitors were taken round, the camera would work for some and not for others, and in the early days George de la Warr could offer no satisfactory explanation.

The operator had to be specially trained to use his apparatus, and a great deal depended on him. Each one had to be trained, and not all developed the necessary skill. The de la Warrs preferred to accept applications from medical students, practitioners and medical auxiliaries who had a basic knowledge on which to build. Those who lived abroad had to visit Britain for training, and one of their most successful pupils was a blind American doctor whose special diagnostic instrument clicked musically when the dials were turned, which enabled it to be set by ear.

An early convert was Foster Cooper, a young doctor who asked whether he could borrow a camera with which to test patients at Bart's. His results were so good that he grew enthusiastic, but after a few weeks orders came from High Authority telling him to remove the offending instrument at once! They had not seen or tested one, but as it was the invention of a layman it could not possibly be any good.

Among those impressed by the camera, however, was Kenneth Walker, Hunterian Professor at the Royal College of Surgeons and a former member of the Medical Research Council; another was a well-known Cambridge physicist. With the endorsement of these two, official bodies such as Naval Intelligence were approached and their experts were sent to have the camera vetted, but as they brought only orthodox knowledge to bear in an entirely new field the results did not come up to their expectations and official recognition was withheld. Even so, a considerable body of medical men rallied to the support of the de la Warrs, and some of these were subsequently trained to use the camera successfully.

The vilification and persecution of the de la Warrs is reminiscent of the way in which Dr T. R. Allinson and Sir Herbert Barker were hounded by the medical profession for their 'unorthodox' views. Allinson defied them and had his licence to practise revoked by his college in Edinburgh; but he was not dismayed and continued to practise, displaying the letters ex-LRCP, LRCS on a brass plate after his name. Barker's medical anaesthetist, Dr F. W. Axham, was struck off and his reputation and career destroyed, but the GMC had no power over Barker, who eventually was honoured by a knighthood.

Four New Laws of Physics *

In 1950 the de la Warrs and their staff lectured at a Scientific and Technical Congress on Radionics and Radiesthesia in London on four new laws of physics:

(1) The Fundamental Energy of the Universe, in the form of energy particles, manifests itself through any energy-pattern which modulates it according to a law of Harmonics.

(2) All forms of matter radiate in a combined wave-form of energy which forms a *force-field* body due to the interaction of inherent radiations.

(3) The *force-field* body is related to the atomic structure and acts in a complex frame aerial through which Fundamental Energy duly manifests itself as matter.

(4) The modulation wave-form depending on space-time considerations can have wave characteristics.

The Field of Agriculture

When treated by radionics orchards of fruit and fields of vegetables have grown faster than others not so treated; and by using aerial photographs 30,000 acres of diseased or infected trees were restored to health.

The de la Warrs have proved that 'thought forms' exist and, though real, have no positive mass. Their mass is negative. Ten thousand photographic exposures of people have revealed the thoughts in their minds!

THOUGHT PHOTOGRAPHY

This is based on the theory that thoughts, which consist of

* See Langston Day in collaboration with George de la Warr, *New Worlds Beyond The Atom* (E. P. Publishing, 1973).

vibrations, are material and like all material objects leave impressions. The earliest pioneer in this field was probably Professor Fukari, a Japanese, who in the presence of a large audience in the Arakawa Theatre produced a dozen dry plates with the seals unbroken that had been bought locally. Four images were suggested to Koichi Mita, a medium, who impressed them on the plates by gazing into the lens for one minute. Further demonstrations took place and in 1928 Professor Fukari, accompanied by Dr Kenichi Yamamoto, a spiritual healer, visited London and during a seance on 19 September impregnated a number of plates solely by concentrating thoughts.

Many years later Dr Julius Eisenbud, MD, psychiatrist and psychoanalyst, took 'thought photographs' with a polaroid camera, of thoughts projected by a Chicago bellhop named Ted Serios, which were published.* The initial tests were made under the supervision of Curtis Fuller, editor of *Fate* magazine and president of the Illinois Society for Psychical Research.

EDWARD BACH

That all plants radiate vibrations, some of which can heal and others destroy, was proved by Edward Bach (Bach is pronounced as spelt), who practised in Harley Street and then relinquished allopathy to become pathologist and bacteriologist at the London Homeopathic Hospital. He came to the conclusion that disease is not due to physical causes but has its origin in the mind; this long before Dr Hans Selye formed the same impression. He did not label the cause of disease 'psychosomatic' but said: 'Treat the patient's personality,' just as physicians of *ayurvedic* medicine in India have done for centuries. Bach said that there were thirty-eight outstanding states of mind from which the sick suffer and if these are banished health will return.

* See Julius Eisenbud, *The World of Ted Serios* (Jonathan Cape, 1968).

Bach was a Psychic

Bach was a highly sensitive man. When he placed his hands over a bowl of flowers he could feel the radiations they emitted. At first his healing tinctures were compounded by pestle and mortar in the homeopathic way, but after long observation he devised a new and better method. He would wander in the fields surrounding his home in Sotwell-cum-Brightwell, Berkshire, and gather petals with the dew on them. Then he would fill a small bowl with water from a nearby spring and float the petals on the surface. The bowl would be placed in the sun for three or four hours to be charged with 'life-giving' force, after which the water would be poured into a vessel and topped with brandy, which Bach found to be the best preserving medium. This he called his Essence. When a remedy was needed a stock bottle was prepared by putting two drops of the Essence into a one-ounce bottle of brandy. Medicines were made up in bottles containing two drops from the stock bottle and one ounce of spring water and this was administered to the patient.

Tinctures of Flowers

Bach had tinctures for all sorts of diseases. One day a man crippled with arthritis hobbled into his surgery complaining that he also suffered from constipation and bleeding piles. He said he had haunted doctors' surgeries without obtaining relief. Bach gave him gorse for hopelessness, red chestnut for anxiety, pine for self-blame, vervain for intensity and overstrain, centaury for weakness, mimulus for nervousness and impatiens for irascibility.

Within a month he was free from pain and could walk without the aid of sticks. His constipation was an affliction of the past and in a year he was walking five miles a day with enjoyment.

The Twelve Healers

After considerable experiment Bach discovered his first twelve healing plants: agrimony, centaury, cerato, chicory, clematis, gentian, impatiens, mimulus, rock rose, scleranthus, vervain and water violet, and wrote about them.* He found that gorse was the remedy for patients who had been ill for so long that they had given up all hope of recovery, and heather for those who feared loneliness and liked to be surrounded by people. He continued finding new preparations till the list grew to thirty-eight.

Before prescribing he investigated the state of mind which produced vibrations that caused the disease, and then applied the various remedies which produced the vibrations for curing them. Almost from the start he attracted disciples from all over the world, who now practise his methods, many of them medical men. For those who cannot make up their own tinctures there are at least two chemists in London who supply them at reasonable cost.

Forbidden to Advertise

In order to spread news of his treatment Bach wrote articles for newspapers and magazines, but because these had to be vetted by staff doctors, most of them were turned down. He decided then to place advertisements in provincial dailies, hoping to bring his methods to the notice of the public, though he was well aware that by doing so he was contravening the medical code. To him, however, the welfare of the sick was paramount. Of the first four, two were accepted, and two returned with the warning that he might get himself into trouble.

Within a very short time the GMC wrote to ask whether the advertisements had been placed by him, and when he admitted they were, asked for an explanation. He replied that all herbs used by him were known to the medical profession and his sole aim was to relieve suffering. The GMC informed him that he would be struck off if he did not cease forthwith, but he continued to advertise – and they did nothing. Hundreds of 'incurables' flocked to the little Berkshire village to be cured

---

* Edward Bach, *The Twelve Healers* (C. W. Daniel, 1933).

after orthodox medicine had failed them, and they in turn spread the good tidings to relatives and friends.

Bach died in 1936, but 'Bach Healers' flourish in a score of countries, some as far afield as New Zealand, Australia, South Africa and South America. Those who knew Bach say he was the kindest man they had ever met.

EMOTIONS PRODUCE DISEASE VIBRATIONS

Bach believed that all emotions set up vibrations. Good emotions, such as love and the desire to please and help, produce good health. Evil emotions, like hate and jealousy, cause disease. They are the origin and basis of all disease.

Greed leads to a desire for power and a denial of freedom and liberty for others. Pride results in arrogance and a rigidity of mind and produces suffering of the limbs. Pain is often the result of acting cruelly. The penalties of hate are loneliness, a violent and uncontrollable temper, mental nerve storms and hysteria. Love of self robs life of much of its enjoyment and causes neurosis, neurasthenia and similar conditions. It is all in keeping with the Law of Cause and Effect, which the yogis call karma, and the Law of Manu states: 'When there is too much evil-doing on the earth the aura of the earth is poisoned and reacts in floods, earthquakes, volcanic eruptions, explosions and extremes of heat and cold.' This may seem far-fetched, but all these conditions exist today.

The very rich who use their vast wealth purely for vulgar aggrandizement or merely to enjoy themselves are never really happy. They marry often but command no love; have many acquaintances but no real friends; imagine that money is the golden key to happiness but fail to realize that all they can buy with it are more and more material things.

That vibrations have physical power has been proved. Kirlian photographs were taken of a highly psychic woman who by merely passing her hands over small objects could move them. They revealed an aura of light encircling her body, which expanded and contracted rhythmically, and a ray of light shooting out of her eyes.

HEALING BY HAND

Experiments carried out in America, the USSR, France and Britain show that psychics are 'power houses' of bioplasmic energy. There are thousands of them scattered throughout the world who cure the halt and lame, or alleviate pain and disease, by passing their hands over affected limbs and organs, or by stroking and massaging them. They are known as 'spiritual' healers, or more often than not as 'faith healers', though they cure the believer and the unbeliever alike, and themselves may belong to no religious body.

Till recently scientists were unable to provide acceptable reasons for such cures, except faith, for as every physician and psychologist knows the mind has the power to kill or cure. The placebo, a word derived from the Latin *placere*, to please, is the doctor's most effective healing agent, for many a medicine is merely coloured and flavoured water, and many a pill is sugar-coated chalk or some harmless substance, but the fact that it has been prescribed by the all-powerful, all-knowing doctor impinges on the patient's mind and usually cures.

We now know, however, that the so-called spiritual healers cure because vibrations projected from their hands pass into the bodies of patients. This is sometimes effective even though the sufferer is miles away and has no physical contact with the healing source. Distant healing proves that thoughts are vibrations, have a material basis, and can be projected.

DR ARNOLD TAYLOR

About twenty-five years ago Dr Arnold Taylor of the Psychosomatic Research Association demonstrated that not only does the human body emit radiations but these vary with the state of health, and can be measured. He amplified and projected these radiations in wave form from an oscilloscope on to a glass screen. The wave form of tuberculosis, for instance, was calibrated on the screen but was deflected when a bottle of tubercular milk was passed in front of the deflector.

He claimed that 95 per cent of his experiments were accurate and showed that *thought resonated* with any object thought about, and threw a beam which could be interpreted directionally.

Father Glazewski, a Polish priest living in Britain, also designed a similar apparatus, and when demonstrated to a number of distinguished investigators his oscilloscope registered simple thought forms on a screen. Working independently and in a different field from the de la Warrs, these two investigators arrived at the same conclusions.

THOUGHTS CAN BLOCK DISEASE

Paul Ellesworth, the American writer, relates a story about a woman his father – a doctor – went to see. She was sallow, emaciated, with eyes sunk deep in their sockets. Her husband said she had been suffering for a year from 'stomach trouble'. On examination Dr Ellesworth found the abdomen so filled with a hard growth that the organs were badly crowded. He wanted to take her husband into another room to break the bad news but the woman quickly stopped him.

'Doctor, is it cancer?' she asked.

Ellesworth hesitated. 'It probably is.'

'Will I die? Tell me the truth.'

'Possibly,' he said. 'But the condition has gone too far for me to operate. If, however, you telegraph to Chicago for Mr X (he named a famous surgeon), who is the best in the country, you have a slim chance.'

The women then turned to her husband. 'John,' she said, 'I have no choice. I forgive you.' She had been nursing a grudge against him for his misbehaviour with another woman.

When Ellesworth went to see her next day she was sitting up in bed, eating ravenously. The growth in her abdomen had vanished. The following day she was up and walking about and within a fortnight she was completely healed. The grudge she nursed had engendered evil thoughts and hatred towards her husband which had been dissipated by her forgiveness. The block to healing vibrations was removed and the way back to health opened.

EGRIGORS

Egrigors, or *tulpas* as they are called in Tibet, are forms created by human thoughts. The yogis believe that thoughts consist of some form of energy and when projected by the mind produce a reflection in the astral plane, remaining there for a period until removed by other thoughts. If the thoughts are evil they can be removed only by kind and helpful thoughts. These thoughts and the emotions they generate take on colours such as blues and fine yellows for beautiful thoughts, and black, reddish-brown and certain shades of green for anger, despair, hatred and jealousy. Such thoughts sometimes take earth forms, and that is why alcoholics and drug addicts see snakes and devils, which doctors call hallucinations, but make no attempt to explain. Something happens in the mind which makes them project thoughts which can be seen; what this is remains to be discovered.

In the same way the minds of people who have suffered long and exhausting illnesses are sometimes so affected that they can see the forms of relatives or friends who have died. Sometimes egrigors are created by curses pronounced in moments of mad rage, or when a victim is being tortured or hanged for something he has not done. Such curses pursue their persecutors, and sometimes their families, for generations. This idea may border on the realms of the fantastic but it has a kernel of truth and should be investigated, for when dealing with the mind one is working in an area of the fantastic.

THE CASE OF ANNA KINGSFORD

This remarkable woman studied under Claude Bernard* in Paris but was so sickened by the vivisection rooms and the cruelty and detachment with which scientists treated living creatures that she willed Bernard's death and then turned her powerful will against Pasteur. This unfortunately had a boomerang effect, for in a letter found after her death she had written: 'I see now that my projections in London against Pasteur were successful. They produced a decided effort of the kind I intended. But they were the main cause of my own illness.' She died a year after that was written.

Her diary records: 'I do not know that much would be gained by recording here the suffering through which I have passed. Whether I brought it on myself occultly by means of my projections against Pasteur, which not being sufficiently strongly impelled or skilfully directed, recoiled on myself – a supposition which I have some grounds for thinking probably correct – matters not very much.'†

Harmful thoughts should never be directed against individuals, but against evil principles.

SISTER JUSTA SMITH

Investigators should aim at objectivity. They should not try to adjust facts to fit preconceived theories. Sister Justa Smith, a Franciscan nun who is Assistant Director of Education at Rosewall Park Memorial Institute (Cancer Research) in Buffalo, New York, and Director of Research for the Human Dimensions Institute, believes that there is some force inside the body which controls healing and the growth and repair of tissues and organs. All healing functions take place involuntarily without any conscious action on the part of the

---

* First professor of Experimental Physiology at the Sorbonne, who discovered that the liver stores glucose in the form of glycogen and releases it when needed; founder of experimental medicine.

† Ed Maitland, *Anna Kingsford* (G. Redway, 1896).

patient. Even the most eminent physicians can do no more than assist Nature, said Osler in *Principles and Practice of Medicine*, the most widely read of all American medical textbooks.

Colonel Estebany

Sister Justa learnt that Dr Bernard Grady of McGill University had discussed his work with a Hungarian healer, Colonel Estebany. This set her thinking. If Estebany could heal, she reasoned, he must by some means be able to stimulate enzyme* activity in the body, for efficient functioning of the body is related to the balance of the enzyme systems in the body, and any healing process must depend on the metabolic reactions of each cell catalyzed by an enzyme.

So Sister Justa persuaded Estebany to cooperate with her in a series of experiments. In one Estebany was asked to hold a vial containing a solution of the enzyme trypsin in a weak mixture of hydrochloric acid and water, and the activity rate of the enzyme was measured to see if the vibrations emitted by the healer's body altered this rate. She found that they did. In another experiment the enzyme was first damaged by ultraviolet radiation before being added to the solution and Estebany was asked if he could heal it. He succeeded.

This proved that rays emitted by him affected enzyme activity in human cells and restored them to health.

She then tried to measure with a gaussmeter whether his hands produced a magnetic field, but this sensitive instrument failed to record any activity.

Nutritional Needs

Sister Justa, like all nutritionists and dieticians, believes that every cell in the body has its own nutritional needs and during illness must be deficient in one or more of these. So she decided to subject vitamin C, which Nobel Prize Winner Linus

---

* An organic substance produced by living cells which act as catalysts. They are proteins, often containing minerals and/or vitamins.

Pauling claims is instrumental in warding off colds and infections, to a test. By means of a technique known as paper chromatography she tested vitamin C produced from natural sources, and also ascorbic acid, which chemists say is identical.

In this the substance being tested leaves distinctly coloured shapes on filter paper. The natural vitamin C produced rays emanating from the centre and a fluted perimeter, whereas the synthetic vitamin merely left a pattern of concentric circles, showing that it lacked some substance possessed by the natural vitamin.

DR CARL SIMONTON

Dr Carl Simonton, chief of Radiation Therapy at David Grant USAF Medical Center, Travis Air Force Base, California, believes that the mind and the emotions it produces play a significant part in health and disease, especially in diseases such as cancer, and set out to prove this now widely held theory.

In 1969 he realized that some patients were unexpectedly cured though the odds against recovery were long, and on probing found that these patients had a strong desire or motive for living – either to see some event for which they had longed take place, or some good fortune happening to some member of the family.

He kept himself informed about the progress of such patients and tuned in his electronic apparatus to their disease – usually cancer – picking up dead and dying cells. In a period of two years during which he 'tuned in' to 152 patients, he proved that his theory was sound, but another three years were to pass before he made definite claims.

Now both he and Sista Justa believe that spiritual disciplines, such as meditation and yoga practice, affect that part of the brain which operates what we call 'the mind' and can make a significant contribution to health and all healing processes.

ECTOPLASM

There is much about the human body and the way it works that we do not know. When mediums first produced ecto-plasm, for instance, scientists scoffed and called them frauds, and indeed many were, and some were caught while produc-ing veils of muslin which they had hidden in secret pockets. But there were also genuine mediums who extruded a subtle living matter capable of assuming liquid, vaporous or even solid states through pores or through the orifices. Some re-searchers noticed that during performances the temperature of seance rooms fell dramatically.

Dr Dombrowski

As long ago as 1916 Dr Dombrowski of the Polish Society for Psychical Research analysed a sample of ectoplasm and pro-duced a bacteriological report which stated: 'The substance is albuminoid matter accompanied by fatty matter and cells in the human organism. Starch and sugar, discovered by Fehling's test, are absent.'

If visible and vaporous ectoplasm can be produced by mediums, what then is the catalyst which enables this to take place? Is it an enzyme or some form of electrical energy? And are enzymes in some way responsible for the generation of electrical energy, or force-fields, in the human body? This is an area awaiting exploration.

4

The Power
of Colour Vibrations

Delve back into the history of civilization and one finds that colours have always played an important part in the customs, rituals and ceremonies of people. Astrology, which is as old as civilization, links the planets with colours: Saturn with black, grey, dark green and brown (especially dark brown); Jupiter with blue; Mars with red; Sun with orange; Moon with blue and violet.

The early Christian Church had colour sequences for certain of its services, such as the Black Canons of the Latin Church of the Holy Sepulchre in Jerusalem, which originated at the start of the twelfth century. Blue was the colour ordained for Ascension Day,* and the Jupiterian blue relates to the resurrection from earth to some empyrean realm beyond the stratosphere.

THE INDIAN CASTE SYSTEM

In Ancient India the caste system was divided into four main

* *An Introduction to English Liturgical Colours*, Sir Walter John Hope and G.C.F. Atchley, pp. 27–9 (SPCK, 1918).

groups; each section having a *varna* or colour. That of the Brahmins (twice born), or priests, was white, which stood for purity and saintliness. Red was the colour of the Kshatriyas or leaders, consisting mainly of soldiers and police. Yellow was that of the Vaisyas whose mental gifts contributed to the prosperity of the nation: merchants, businessmen, farmers and traders. Black was the colour of the Sudras, who toiled and performed menial duties.

ANCIENT TIBET

In Tibet, where till recently life was unchanged from that in the Middle Ages, the north was yellow, the south blue, and east and west were white and red respectively. In Ancient Ireland the north was black, the south white, the east purple and the west brown. In China the north was black, the south red, the east green and the west white. The Navajo Indians of America say that the north is black, the south blue, and the east and west yellow and purple. How people arrived at such conclusions is not known, but there must have been some basis for their beliefs.

ARISTOTLE COLOURED THE ELEMENTS

Aristotle associated the elements with colours. According to him air, water and earth were white, fire and sun yellow. But to the ancient Chinese the earth was yellow, water black, fire red, wood green and metal white.

Most people have a feeling for colours, and more often than not their likes and dislikes are closely related to the planets under which they were born. This would have been described as utter nonsense by scientists a century ago, but now we have begun to realize that there exists an affinity between Man and the Universe. In the Victorian and Edwardian eras people were reluctant to use bright colours, and even pastel shades were considered 'daring'. The interiors of homes were papered in sombre hues, browns, greys and dark green predominating, reflecting the mentality of the people and influencing their outlook. Only the gay and feckless Latins and the lesser breeds in Asia and Africa splashed their surroundings with bright colours and bedecked themselves gaily to raise their spirits.

THE YOGIS AND COLOURS

As far as we know the first people to link colours with human well-being were the yogis. By means of special breathing exercises (*pranayama*) and postures (*asanas*) they acquired extrasensory perception which enabled them to see, hear and feel vibrations which normal people did not. They could see the human aura in all its colours, and those of the *chakras* or centres of nervous power. The colour of the anus is orange; navel green; heart yellow; spleen almost rainbow; throat violet-blue speckled with pink and yellow; and that of a healthy body as a whole, rose pink. By the control of breath they aroused *kundalini* (psychic energy), which enabled them to see these colours in the various stages of development.

Every phase of Indian life is linked with colours, which are regarded as essential to health and the development of the personality.

COLOURS OF THE AURA

The aura changes colour in health and in sickness and also according to the way one lives and thinks, for over the years thoughts can change the expression of the face and the condition and functioning of the organs.

Black in an aura is the colour of hatred, malice, envy, revenge; it is not without reason that we speak of 'black hatred'.

Bright grey represents selfishness and *dull grey* a fear of death, terror and cowardice.

Dark grey, the nearest colour to black, represents melancholy, depression and hopelessness.

Dull green indicates that the wearer of this aura is jealous, and in conversation one speaks of him as being 'green with jealousy'. If green is speckled with red it shows that anger accompanies jealousy.

Slate-green is a sign that the person is mean and deceitful.

Bright green, however, means that the aura envelops a tolerant, easy-going, adaptable, tactful subject, polite and wise in a worldly sense, but who has a tendency, like the Vicar of Bray, to adjust his principles to changing conditions.

Dull green tinged with a touch of grey denotes animal passion.

Bright red indicates flashes of anger, and on a black background means that the anger is engendered by hatred, malice and envy. If on a greenish background it means that the person is riddled with jealousy. If, however, the emotion is one of righteous anger only red flashes will appear and there will be no background.

Crimson is the colour of love. If the love is gross and earthy the colour will be dull, for the higher forms of love result in more pleasing shades and the highest form of all – unselfish love – is shown when the body is suffused by a lovely shade of rose.

Brown tinged with red means that the subject is greedy and grasping.

Orange denotes ambition and the pride which flows from it.

Yellow is a good colour, for it represents the intellect. If the intellect is poor the hue will be dull and dark but will grow brighter if the intellect is developed. In the case of an exceptionally powerful intellect which is harnessed for the betterment of mankind it will shine with a brilliant gold.

Blue is the colour of religious feeling and outlook. If tinged with selfishness, as it often is, it will change to full indigo. The higher the emotion the richer will be the colour, and those with the highest religious feeling, who are devoted to helping the poor and dying, such as Mother Theresa, have rich violet auras.

Light blue reflects spirituality, and the higher the type the more luminous and filled with light will the colour be. The saints are said to have auras which sparkle like stars in a snow scene.

COLOURS OF THE ZODIAC

Planet	Sign	Colours
Sun	Leo	Orange and gold
Moon	Cancer	White, silver and opal
Neptune	Pisces	Mauve
Uranus	Aquarius	Checks, stripes and greens
Saturn	Capricorn	Black and dark brown
Jupiter	Sagittarius	Violet and purple
Mars	Aries	Red and crimson
Venus	Taurus and Libra	Blues, pinks and turquoise
Mercury	Gemini and Virgo	Bright yellow and indigo
Pluto	Scorpio	Sparkling or metallic black

This is not as fanciful as it may seem, for if you question friends and acquaintances you will find that those born under the signs shown are likely to favour the corresponding colours. Where this is not so it will be found that the native is born on the cusp of the sign; that is, on one extreme to the sign adjoining.

All this was relegated to the realms of mumbo-jumbo and eastern superstition till men like Goethe, Reichenbach, Reich, Steiner, Kilner, Jung and others formulated their theories and proved scientifically that colours and the planets influence human behaviour and health.

THE NAMING OF COLOURS
AND THEIR SYMBOLISM

In all probability some colours were named after flowers, minerals and gems; rose, heliotrope, violet, orange, lemon, gold, silver, copper, opal, turquoise, ruby, emerald, sapphire, amber, etc.

In different parts of the world colours have a different significance. White was worn by the Vestal Virgins in ancient Rome as proof of their innocence and virtue, and that is why it is still worn by the majority of brides when they marry in church. In India and China, however, it is the colour of mourning, for death is not considered a reason for sorrow but is regarded as the release of the soul from the prison of the body and an occasion for rejoicing.

Yellow is the royal colour in China, whereas in India it symbolizes intellect, and in the West purple is the royal colour.

In Japan red symbolizes fire and destruction, in India protection from disease, in the West it is the colour of danger, and after 1917 the colour of Communism and general upheaval.

COLOURS AND MOODS

Moods are so strongly influenced by colours that phrases embodying them have crept into our language. We speak of the black mood of depression and call Black Monday the day of the week on which most people start work, or return to work after holidays. We describe a person in a blinding rage as 'seeing red'. We contemplate in a 'brown study', are 'blue' when in the dumps, turn 'green with envy', and 'scarlet with embarrassment'. Cowards are stigmatized as being 'yellow'; being 'off-colour' denotes a sate of indifferent health; and a rascal exposed is seen in his 'true colours'. Optimists see life through 'rose-coloured glasses'; people turn 'white with fear', and so on.

COLOUR-BLINDNESS

In 1977 Huddart became the first person to draw attention to colour-blindness, but that such a condition existed was questioned by scientists at the time, who refused to believe that unfortunates existed who could not distinguish red from green.

Then in 1794 Sir John Dalton, the distinguished chemist who formulated the Atomic Theory, was the first scientist to prove that he was colour-blind, and by so doing caused a stir. He was a Quaker, and Quakers were noted for their predilection for drab colours and dislike of gay hues. Yet on receiving his degree of doctor of civil law he strode about the streets of Oxford in his scarlet gown for several days, happily unconscious of the effect he produced. Physiologists investigated his case and the name Daltonism was given to those who could not distinguish red from green.

Deuteranopes and Protanopes

Not all colour-blind people are the same. Some can distinguish between certain colours and not others, and no more than a hundred cases have been found where the only colours seen are black, grey and white. Most colour deficiencies involve only a confusion between red and green, and in this category there are two types. Colour-blind people who see grey in place of both red and green with the relative brightness of the colours unchanged are known as *deuteranopes*. A few have their colour vision further complicated by a shift of relative brightness away from the long wavelengths towards the short wavelengths, so that instead of red they see black, and instead of green they see a whitish-grey. These are known as *protanopes*.

Colour-blindness affects about 4 per cent of men in Great Britain and about 0.4 per cent of women, and though the defect is rarer in women they can pass it on to their children. It is cogenital and, as far as we know, incurable. Scientists believe it depends on the nerve connections of the cones in the eye as well as the cones themselves. Colour-blindness may not be as inhibiting as it seems, for colour, like beauty, is in the eye of the beholder.

SIR ISAAC NEWTON

Sir Isaac Newton was the first scientist to show that a beam of colourless light could be split into the colours of the rainbow (violet, indigo, blue, green, yellow, orange and red) by passing it through a prism. Logically it seemed to him that colour must be a property of light itself. Since his day physicists have shown that the luminous spectrum is only a small part of the whole spectrum of radiation, which extends from the long radio waves ($18\frac{1}{2}$ miles) through the infrared to the visible light waves, and on to the shorter waves of the ultraviolet and X-rays, and to the microscopic cosmic radiation (4 ten-trillionths of an inch).

In 1704 Newton laid down the first two laws governing the mixing of colour stimuli. The third law was established about a hundred years ago; but these do not concern us.

Colours may be softened into shades, which are colours of small luminosity, and then into bright or dull tints, as shown in the table below:

Pure Hues	Shades	Bright Tints	Dull Tints
Red	Maroon	Salmon Pink	Flesh Colour
Orange	Brown	Cream	Fawn
Yellow	Orange	Straw	Khaki
Green	Myrtle	Apple Green	Reseda
Turquoise	Peacock	Aquamarine	Gobelin Blue
Ultramarine	Navy	Sky Blue	Butcher Blue
Violet	Plum	Heliotrope	Lavender Grey
Magenta	Claret	Rose-Pink	Vieux-Rose

VIBRATIONS

Every hue, shade and tint has a different vibration in the same way as sunlight, ultraviolet, infrared, X-rays or cosmic rays. When a strip of metal or a stretched wire is made to vibrate, the human ear is able to hear the lowest note it can register. The more rapid the rate of vibration, the higher the note, till at 36,000 vibrations a minute the hearing apparatus no longer responds.

COLOUR VIBRATIONS

Colour vibrations are not like ordinary white light or sound vibrations. They are ether vibrations, and when we see violet, for instance, it is because vibrations enter our eyes at 780,000,000 a second at one end of the spectrum, and at 450 trillions a second at the other end when we see red. Below and above these levels there are no colours that the human eye can distinguish. All the rest are light rays, such as ultraviolet, which if gazed at for more than a few seconds can seriously impair or even destroy sight unless special tinted spectacles are worn. Red light rays are one three-hundred-thousandth of an inch in length and violet rays one six-hundred-thousandth of an inch.

Radiations are characteristic not only of people but of rooms, houses, streets and even towns, and it is these that provide what is known as an 'atmosphere'. On entering a strange house where a gruesome murder has been committed a sensitive person can instantly feel the atmosphere prevailing.

COLOURS IN HEALING

Anyone intending to take up chromotherapy, or to use the American term, colour engineering, must master the art of harmonizing colours; the contrasts which exist between the hues; the complementary colours; warm colours and cold; their luminosity or tone, and the use of black, white and grey in colour schemes. All warm colours contain a percentage of yellow, which can be increased by the use of gold; silver harmonizes with cold colours and contrasts with those that are warm.

Colours such as red, orange and yellow and their related tints and shades have a stimulating effect on the mind and body. Blue and green are soothing and violet is depressing. White invariably cheers but blacks and greys are sombre and depressing.

It would be impossible to mention every hue, shade and tint

for according to Dr R. E. Rose, a former director of the Organic Chemicals Department of E. I. Du Pont de Nemours & Co., of Wilmington, Delaware, a well-trained eye can detect the difference in more than 100,000 colours and shades! The average untrained person can distinguish only between about 160 colours, shades and tints in sunlight.

Health is not simply a matter of bodily well-being but of harmony of body, mind and spirit. Usually, though we do not realize it, the state of the mind affects the spirits, and if the spirits are constantly low illness is round the corner. Most people think of their bodies as the key to health but in actual fact it is the other way round. A person who is constantly cheerful and happy and can laugh heartily is rarely ill. The key to health is a contented mind.

Disease is precisely what it spells: DIS-EASE. It is a departure from the normal vital or physiological functions of living organisms, or a disturbance of natural functions resulting in discomfort, pain or inability to live a normal existence.

Underlying pathological conditions there is *usually* a psychic condition which is the primary cause of disease. This psychic condition may be emotional and is usually caused by fear, worry, anxiety, hatred, jealousy, disappointment, repression, inhibition, a deep-rooted sense of injustice, or sexual troubles.

Constant embarrassment, which sensitive people suffer, may eventually lead to physical illness, as it causes disturbances of the blood, usually in the face, but sometimes throughout the body. Often one hears a woman say: 'I went hot and cold all over,' yet few think that blushing, caused by frequent embarrassment, may be a prelude to physical illness.

Violent passion has the same effect but to a much greater degree. One can see the veins in the temples of a man in a rage throbbing as the blood courses through them, and those in the neck swelling when rage is uncontrollable.

Disappointment, despondency, sorrow – all three can cause illness or accelerate it if illness is already present. Neville Chamberlain, for instance, was so disappointed when his judgement and confidence in Hitler was proved wrong and all his hopes and plans for peace doomed to failure that he relinquished the will to live and died soon after of cancer. He fell from power on 10 May 1940 and on 16 June his diary recorded that for the first time he had 'considerable pain in the abdomen'. On the 24th X-rays revealed a partial stricture of the bowel and an exploratory operation was ordered. On 9 September he returned to Downing Street 'a partially crippled man'.* He resigned from office on 3 October and died on 9 November.

Nearly twenty years later Sir Heneage Ogilvie, the famous surgeon, wrote: 'The happy man never gets cancer. The instances where the first recognizable onset of cancer has followed almost immediately on some disaster, bereavement, the break-up of a relationship, a financial crisis, or an accident are so numerous that they suggest that some controlling force that had hitherto kept the outbreak in check has been removed.'† Despondency has caused many a suicide, and the loss of a marriage partner after a lifetime of happiness often destroys the will to live of the survivor.

VIBRATIONS OF DISEASE

The vibrations of a healthy person may be recorded on a clinical thermometer in terms of heat. In health temperature varies between 92.2° and 98.4°F. A rise or fall in the rate of vibrations results in the rise or fall in body-heat, and a difference of half a degree is sufficient to upset the balance. As much as seven degrees is usually fatal. When the balance is upset one feels 'out of sorts' or 'off-colour', and a doctor is summoned. He prescribes a drug or an antibiotic to fight the germ or virus which he thinks is present. This alters the rate of vibration and gives the subconscious a chance to restore the body to health. More often than not rest and an abstinence from food will restore vitality more effectively than drugs.

* Iain McLeod, *Neville Chamberlain* (Muller, 1961).
† Sir Heneage Ogilvie, *The Human Heritage* (Max Parrish).

What happens is this: the drugged organs react and try to expel the drug or drugs, which they do by increasing or decreasing the rate of vibrations, in which case side-effects often result. Many drugs are uncertain in action and much depends on the psychic make-up of the patient.

All cures are ultimately self-cures. What drugs *sometimes* do is to help; more often than not, however, they interfere with the rate of vibrations. What is needed is a school of preventive medicine such as existed in ancient China, where physicians were paid as long as patients remained in health, and all treatment during illness was free.

COLOURS HEAL

The temples of healing in ancient Greece were havens of light and colour, and as music was used in conjunction with colour the combination had a beneficial psychological effect. The Greeks knew what happened but they did not know why. They had no 'scientific' proof.

NIELS FINSEN THE LIGHT-HUNTER

The first man scientifically to investigate light and colour was Niels Finsen, an Icelandic medical student. About a hundred years ago he watched a cat basking on a roof just below his room. As the sun journeyed on its way west a shadow from a nearby wall fell on the cat, which then moved into the sun. Again and again this happened, which made Finsen ask himself whether it was just for warmth or also for some other reason. He knew that animals instinctively did what was good for them. They fasted when ill, rested when tired or injured, immersed broken or bruised limbs in running streams, ate grass when they needed it, and lay in the sun. He decided to find out whether there was some element in sunshine that was beneficial to the body, apart from heat.

So he painted a band of Indian ink on one arm and exposed the arm to the sun, and his skin grew red and inflamed –

except where it was painted. By some means unknown to him the black band had effectively shut out the rays which burn and blister. That must be the reason, he thought, why Negroes, whose skins are black, can bear tropical sun without discomfort. Nature has provided them with a protective chemical (which we now know is melanin) to absorb the burning rays and tan the skin. He also found that if his arm was tanned gradually the skin did not turn red and blister, and he realized why sailors who were constantly exposed to the sun were tanned and immune.

He was working at the time in the smallpox ward of the Blegdam Hospital in Copenhagen, and wondered whether strong light affected the blisters on his patients, which became inflamed and infected. He put his theory to the chief physician, who merely laughed sardonically, for Finsen had suggested keeping smallpox patients in rooms in which the windows would be covered by thick red curtains, which would let in the red rays of sunlight but shut out the blue, violet and ultraviolet.

Unknown to Finsen, a fourteenth-century English physician, John of Gaddesden, had used scarlet blankets and red wall furnishings in rooms where smallpox patients were quarantined because he found that such precautions prevented their blisters from becoming inflamed and poisoned.

Finsen wrote a paper on his theory and Lindholm and Svendsen, doctors in Bergen, read it. They placed a number of patients into wards behind thick red curtains, and when a fortnight later they were released into daylight their blisters had dried, without leaving the usual disfiguring scars, and they were free from blood poisoning. On the strength of this, Finsen applied for a fellowship to enable him to continue research on sunlight, but was turned down.

He also noticed that in springtime insects, animals and human beings seemed to experience a new surge of life, due to the sun. He then proved that though natural sunlight gave people energy, *concentrated* sunlight killed microbes fifteen times as fast as ordinary sunlight.

The chief engineer of the local electric company was a friend named Morgensen, who suffered from incurable skin tuberculosis, so he persuaded him to design a brilliant arclight which produced a blue flame. This he played, through a set of lenses, on an ulcer on one side of Morgensen's face, and within a few weeks his friend was cured!

This and many other experiments with light and colour earned Finsen a Nobel Prize and encouraged men like Rollier in Switzerland and Ove Strandberg in Sweden to experiment with light and colour rays, curing hundreds of patients and saving lives. They found that sometimes pigmentation of the skin appeared to help it to resist disease; that rashes which afflicted the white portions of patients' bodies did not secure a hold on the pigmented areas; and that skin diseases such as acne and boils were almost unknown among Negroes. They proved that pigmentation is caused by rays of the shortest length in the solar spectrum: from 0.00029 to 0.00033 mm, and if passed through ordinary glass they shorten still further and are absorbed by the glass. They also found that the eye is damaged if exposed to light of long wavelength, and cataract can be caused by red and infrared rays; that blue light has an anaesthetic action, and red light can be used to heal chronic ulcers.

CAMILLE FLAMMARION

Camille Flammarion (1842–1925), who founded the Astronomical Society of France, was among the first to show an interest in colours and their effects on humans. To start with he conducted scores of experiments with coloured lights on young lettuce plants and found that those planted under red glass grew four times as rapidly as those planted in sunlight. Under green glass they grew only slightly quicker than in sunlight; but under blue glass growth was retarded and the plants were stunted.

Next he tried Indian corn, and found that in sunlight his

plants attained a height of 25 inches; under red glass over the same period, 18 inches; and under green, 18 inches. Under blue glass they reached a height of only 8 inches.

Charles Fere was another to investigate the effects of coloured lights on the human body, and showed that activity is stimulated by white light but increases progressively under blue, green, yellow, orange and red respectively. Pressy, also a scientist who researched the effects of colour, found that arithmetical work was carried out more efficiently under red than white light, and Fere and Rand conducted experiments which showed that discomfort and loss of efficiency were caused by reading under lights of different colours.

Colours	Loss of efficiency (per cent)	Feeling of discomfort after
Unsaturated yellow	5.43	116 seconds
Reddish-yellow – more saturated	7.57	94 seconds
Unsaturated yellow with trace of red	8.29	90
Orange yellow	8.39	90
Unsaturated yellow with trace of green	8.48	90
Unsaturated yellow with more green	24.00	48
Unsaturated yellowish-green	25.51	34
Greenish	39.14	21
Bluish-green	58.86	14

EXPERIMENTS IN COLOUR-BLINDNESS

C. J. Birch tried to discover the effects of coloured light on the eye. He focused red glass on the eye and found that after a time the subject became temporarily blind to red. Scarlet poppies seemed black, yellow flowers green, and purple flowers violet.

When white light was passed through violet glass, violet objects seemed black, grass appeared a much richer green, and purple flowers seemed to be crimson.

But if one eye was rendered purple-blind and the other green-blind, all objects appeared in their natural colours but in exaggerated perspective, as the brain found difficulty in coordinating the images from both eyes.

EXPERIMENTS IN A MENTAL HOME

Dr Ponza, Director of the Mental Hospital in Alexandria (Italy), one of the pioneers of light therapy, had windows of coloured glass fitted in certain rooms, and the walls painted the same colours. After consulting Secchi, the astronomer, he used red and violet for the first experiments, and recorded the results. 'The violet glass,' he said, 'has an inexpressibly depressing quality which lowers the spirits of the patients . . . perhaps violet light may calm the excited nerves of the maniac.'

At Secchi's suggestion a violent inmate was placed in a violet room and within twenty-four hours grew calm and normal. Another patient, notorious for his violence, so improved after twenty-four hours in the same room that he was soon released. Nor did he relapse.

The vibrations from red had the opposite effect, and a patient who suffered from taciturn delirium became almost loquacious when made to spend three hours in a red room.

RED—A DANGEROUS COLOUR

It is no accident that red lights and red flags are used as warnings of danger, for an eminent American psychiatrist says that anyone forced to live in a room with red walls and hangings and illuminated by red lamps would go mad within weeks. Red, and colours with a red content, stimulate and excite. The firm of Lumière of Lyons, manufacturers of photographic plates, conducted a number of experiments with lights and found that in their dark rooms, which were illuminated by red lamps, workers grew bad-tempered and quarrelsome and tired quickly, but when put to work in rooms lit by green lamps they were transformed into calm, even-tempered beings who at the end of the day showed little sign of fatigue.

EDWARD PODOLSKY

Dr Edward Podolsky, one of the foremost authorities on colour in America, said: 'The right colours and colour combinations in our homes, offices, shops, travel accommodations and hospitals are exceedingly important for health and efficiency . . . injudicious colour combinations can work havoc with our well-being.' According to him, factory owners do not realize how greatly they can increase output by using the right colour combinations. In a Pennsylvania printing shop where the dominant colours had been black, brown and dark green the owner called in a colour engineer who had all the machines painted a rich delf-blue, the pillar bases light grey, the upper portions bright yellow and the ceiling a bright buff. Even the waste cans were bright blue. The drab floor was ripped out and oiled maple substituted, and mahogany tables were bought. The expense was considerable but the workers were much happier, and efficiency so improved that the difference in colours paid off in a very short time and profits shot up dramatically.

Of all the colours red has the greatest effect on muscular activity but can be dangerous if used indiscriminately. Dr Donald Laird of Colgate University, who spent four years studying people's sleeping habits, stated in a report: 'If your body is awake your mind will not sleep. Red in a bedroom may keep you awake, this even though your eyes are closed and the light switched off!' Because of this red should be used very sparingly in bedrooms.

Not everyone is affected by colours in the same way. Obviously the colour-blind are not. The degree to which colours affect people varies considerably. Soon after we married, my wife and I went to view a flat in Chelsea. When we opened the sitting room door we reeled back, for the wallpaper was painted with thick scarlet stripes, making it into a tiger's cage.

'We couldn't possibly live with that paper!' cried my wife, and as those were the days when landlords went down on their hands and knees if you so much as glanced at their property, it was soon redecorated in pastel shades.

Generally speaking, women are more sensitive than men to gradations of colour. Whereas a man will describe a certain colour as *red*, a woman will give the exact shade or tint according to the quantity of red it contains: rose, vermilion, crimson or scarlet; or in the case of *blue*, duck-egg, peacock-blue, turquoise, sapphire, cobalt or aquamarine.

Contrary to expectation, artists are not more conscious about the colour of their surroundings than other people, for they grow so absorbed in their work that they become oblivious to their surroundings. I have known some superb artists to exist in chaos and squalor such as would have demoralized many people, in tasteless, grubby rooms. Their minds were so focused on their work that neither dirt nor clashing colours seemed to affect them. It was what they put on their canvasses that mattered. It would be mistaken, therefore, to make sweeping generalizations about people and colours.

THE EFFECTS OF COLOUR VIBRATIONS ON THE SPIRITS

Even those who have never given the matter a thought admit that sunshine makes an enormous difference to spirits and outlook. When the sun is blanketed in fog spirits tend to sink, but the moment it breaks through and splashes the world in gold our mood changes. Flowers, grass, leaves, houses, gardens, the earth and sky are transformed. That is why holidays in the Mediterranean are so popular; even those who go out and play bingo and eat eggs and chips feel rejuvenated. When the sun comes out the sky is magically painted blue and the malevolent green of the sea changes to ultramarine or deep purple. And in places like Greece, for instance, a rare light suffuses everything.

Even in Britain old brick and stone walls come to life with a dozen different hues. I have picked out a score of colours in old walls on which the sun shone. This happens to a lesser degree in bright moonlight.

THE POWER OF IMAGINATION

This will be put down by some to the power of imagination, but imagination is the greatest aid there is to creation. It is on imagination that the basis of sound medical practice rests, for if the patient imagines that the doctor knows his job, the medicines he takes and the ministrations he receives will chase away his ills, or alleviate them. In his autobiography Graham Greene says that when the first novel he wrote came back after being in the publisher's hands for a year, he sent it to Heinemann and prepared to wait another year. A few days later he went down with flu, and when the phone rang moaned: 'Tell them I'm ill and can't answer.' Then as an afterthought: 'Who is it?'

With her hand on the mouthpiece his wife shouted from downstairs: 'It's a Mr Evans from Heinemann. He wants to speak to you.'

The invalid who a few moments ago had been on his deathbed suddenly remembered that a Mr Evans had sent him a line to acknowledge the receipt of his manuscript. 'Hold on!' he bellowed, and leaping from his bed like an Olympic athlete he raced to the phone. Mr Evans informed him that they had decided to publish his book and would like him to drop in and see them.

Would he! His flu vanished, never to return. He dressed faster than any fireman when 'the bells go down', and was with his publisher within the hour. It was all due to the vibrations which generate imagination, and anyone who scoffs at imagination is a fool. I have seen it work a hundred times.

Eric Blott, an old friend who worked for the Westminster Press Group in Oxford, lay groaning in bed on a summer's day with a virulent attack of flu, much too weak even to raise his head when the phone rang. 'Eric,' said his wife as he lay on his couch of pain, 'they've just phoned to say they're a man short and ask if you could stagger along and help them – but I said you were in bed with flu.'

'What!' he bawled, miraculously resuscitated, 'get back to them at once and tell them I'll be there.' Within minutes he was tossing his cricket bag into the boot of his car and before the tea interval had taken five wickets. Later Doreen Blott remarked somewhat cynically that if her spouse lay in his coffin and someone asked if he could turn out for a game he'd find the strength to push the lid up and crawl out.

I could write a book on the miracles the power of imagination has produced. In some strange way the vibrations of colours act similarly on the mind, stir the imagination and make us well – or, if they are the wrong colours, ill.

THE PENETRATIVE POWER OF LIGHT VIBRATIONS

Few people realize that light rays have considerable penetrative power, which decreases with wavelength. The shorter the wavelength, the greater the penetration. Ordinary light (white light) will barely penetrate the thinnest sheets of gold leaf. X-rays will pass through a fractionally thin sheet of gold or lead, and some other rays will penetrate inches of lead.

Colour is responsible for every sensation made upon the eye. We see shapes, for instance, because of the contrast between one colour and another. Few realize this, but look round your room at the many objects it contains and you will see how true this is. If you look carefully while in the country you will see hundreds of shades and tints in the trees, their bark and foliage, and in the sky and distant hills. The eye, Nature's most wonderful instrument, registers them all in a twinkling.

Nor do most people realize that when they look, for instance, at a red car it appears red because its surface reflects the red rays of white light and absorbs the other colours of the spectrum. If it absorbed them all the car would appear black.

If it reflected them all the car would appear white.

The eye is sensitive only to a narrow band of light rays, but a machine called a *colorcable*, invented by Howard Ketcham, an American, can separate thousands of hues, shades, and tints and transmit them over telegraph and cable lines.

THE COLOUR CIRCLE

In healing, use is made of eight pure colours; that is, the colours of the spectrum, and magenta or ruby, as shown in the circle below.

The left side of the circle contains colours which have a soothing, calming, soporific effect; the right side those which stimulate and excite the nerves, organs and tissues and accelerate their functions. When these colours are mixed the resulting shades have either a more positive or negative effect, depending on the colours with which they are mixed.

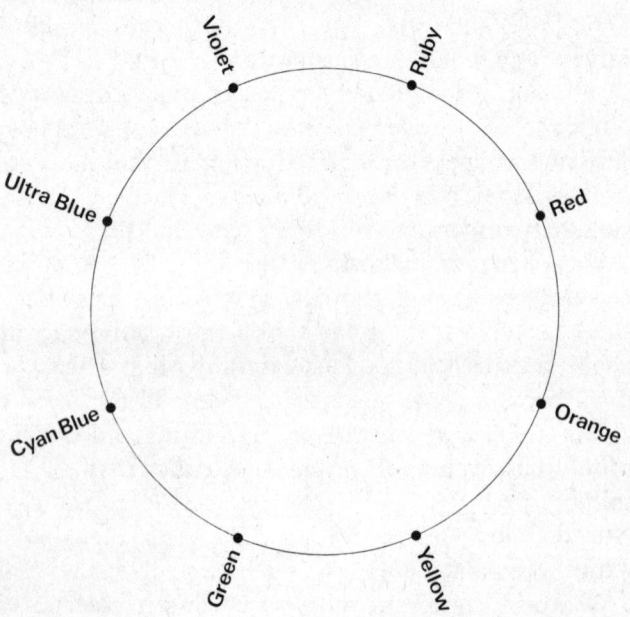

EFFECTS OF COLOURS
ON THE MIND AND NERVES

The vibrations emitted by colours have a distinct effect on the
mind and nerves, depending on the receptivity of the subject.

Violet depresses and has a soporific effect.
Blues are soothing and calming.
Red arouses passions and excites.
Orange also excites, but can irritate.
Yellow stimulates and livens.
Grey is a neutral colour.
White is another stimulating colour.
Black depresses.

Each colour has a symbolical meaning, but to describe them
all would mean digression into the realms of chromo-
psychology.

It has been proved that colours affect pathological conditions and it is to this end that they are applied in chromotherapy.

Violet: not only does violet induce lethargy, melancholia
and sleep but it is a strong bactericide and parasiticide and is
effective on its own, or mingled with ruby, in the treatment of
skin infections and the reduction of pus. We know that ultraviolet rays kill certain types of bacteria and increase the red
blood corpuscles, but as violet depresses it must not be used for
diseases such as rheumatism, gout, forms of paralysis, or any
condition where vitality is low.

Blues: these increase metabolic action and promote the
growth of healthy cells. They are invaluable for the treatment
of excitable people and in cases of high blood pressure and inflammation, but harmful where the patient is sluggish and
lacks vitality. Tests should be made to ensure that when white
light is transmitted through blue glass there is no hint of ruby
in the shade.

Green: this should be neither a bluish nor a yellowish tint
but should be the colour of emerald. Then it will be anti-
inflammatory and effective in the reduction of blood pressure,

hysteria, and will soothe excitable or irritable patients. It is also used in the treatment of jaundice and biliousness.

Red: radiates heat. It is no accident that when in the past homes throughout Britain were damp and draughty, red flannel petticoats were popular. The use was perhaps instinctive. Red has the longest wavelength of the colours in the spectrum and possesses the most powerful thermal property. It raises temperature, stimulates the nervous system and increases metabolism. Because it brings arterial blood to the surface it is invaluable in the treatment of all *eruptive* fevers; but as it animates, excites and irritates it should not be used for normal feverish conditions or inflammation. Nor should red be used on the head, in the treatment of the obese, the red-haired or those with a ruddy complexion.

Orange: this should be the colour of a ripe orange and is often used in conjunction with red, though its heat rays are even more powerful. Orange is good for eruptive fevers but its use should be followed by blue or green.

Yellow: this should be the colour of a ripe lemon. Though lacking the heating property of red it is a powerful stimulant of the mind and nerves and that is why it is known as the colour of the intellect. It is laxative and purgative, and yellow light is often used in the treatment of constipation. It has a beneficial effect on the kidneys, liver, and spleen and is also used for paralysis, severe rheumatism, dropsy and similar conditions. Yellow stimulates the cells of the skin without raising body temperature, the sensory and motor nerves, and the solar plexus. It has many uses for a wide range of ailments, and used alternatively with blue produces a vital rhythm.

Ruby: this is not visible in the spectrum band and differs from the colours of the spectrum. When white light is passed through ruby glass the rays should contain no hint of yellow or violet. Pure ruby glass is rare and usually manganese violet has to be superimposed on copper ruby to get the right hue. Gelatine stained with rhodamine B produces the right effect, though it is liable to fade after long exposure to sunlight.

Ruby acts as a general tonic and stimulates the flow of the

vital forces which the Chinese call *yang* and *yin*, without adversely affecting the nervous system. It helps to promote the formation of haemoglobin, livens the action of the stomach, pancreas, liver, spleen, and kidneys, and like violet it destroys bacteria and parasites. It also improves the circulation and stimulates the growth of hair, nails and skin. Ruby is an excellent tonic for the anaemic and tubercular, and for patients whose energy has been depleted. It also relieves gastric troubles.

To those who know nothing about chromotherapy such claims may seem riduculous, but results have proved the effectiveness of colours in healing.

THE CASE OF GORDON TURNER

Gordon Turner, who has cured hundreds of people by 'laying on his hands', describes* how after he had strained his back playing rugger, an ancient of 97 years, who said he had been a colour healer and astrologer, offered to treat him after the doctors had failed to give him any relief. Turner did not take him seriously, but as he was in considerable pain agreed to be his patient.

The old man produced several lengths of coloured muslin from capacious pockets and murmured: 'Red. Yes, red for pain,' then paused: 'a little green to relax the muscles, and yellow for the nerves. . .'

He draped his patient's back with red muslin, then bending over him blew violently to dissipate bad vibrations. Red was followed by green and finally by yellow – again with much puffing and blowing. After which the ancient, exhausted by his exertions, slumped into a chair and was so breathless that he could hardly sip the reviving cup of tea that was pushed into his trembling hands. When rested, he assured Turner that his trouble would be clear in next to no time.

Turner was incredulous but only when he was slipping into

* Gordon Turner, *A Time To Heal* (Franklin Talmy, 1974).

bed that night did he realize that the pain in his back was no
more! He never saw the old man again to thank him.

COLOUR THERAPY

Though all the colours in the spectrum, together with magenta,
are used in chromotherapy, the most important are red,
yellow and blue. Nor are colours always used in their pure
form. Often they are mixed; sometimes the use of one colour is
followed by another. As with all healing treatments the practitioner has to learn not only what effects the colours have,
but how they affect different types of people.

In colour healing *harmony* is said to exist when tints are
used in conjunction with bright hues or shades and tints of
bright hues: for instance, green, myrtle, apple-green or
reseda; or violet, plum, heliotrope and lavender-grey.

Disharmony is said to exist when pure hues within a few degrees of each other are used: for instance, orange and orange-
red; or yellow and yellow-green. Disharmony can, however,
be diminished if some neutral colour such as black, grey,
silver, gold or white separates them.

Pure colours are said to be in *contrast* when colours on the
circle more than 90 degrees apart are used together; for
instance, ruby and yellow, or violet and orange.

Colours are said to be *complementary* if when superimposed by lantern projection they produce white, or if when
mixed with pigments in the right proportions they produce
black. The four principal contrast pairs are red and turquoise-
blue, orange and ultramarine, yellow and violet, and green
and magenta.

Bad combinations are formed by two pure hues situated less
than 90 degrees apart on the colour circle, such as orange and
yellow, or violet and ultramarine. Their effect may be modified by the addition of some warm colour; that is, one containing yellow.

Luminosity is obtained when two bright hues such as red
and green are in juxtaposition by introducing shades of these

two elements and substituting myrtle for green and salmon for red.

Contrast of luminosity is achieved when bright hues are placed in juxtaposition, or when their hues or tints are adjacent.

Black, grey and white, together with gold and silver, are treated as neutral elements in colour combinations. Black does not combine well with cold colours, or blues, greens and various shades and tints of these colours, but it does with warm colours such as yellows and reds. The same principle applies to grey.

White harmonizes with all colours.

Gold harmonizes with all warm colours and contrasts with the cold ones.

Silver harmonizes with all cold colours and contrasts with the warm ones.

GENERAL RULES

In Nature pure colours are confined almost entirely to flowers, butterflies, birds and certain species of fish. Elsewhere one finds colour combinations of shades and tints.

On surfaces where paint is applied, it will vary in contrast and luminosity according to the angles from which light falls on them, the degree of sunlight, the amount of cloud or sky visible, the colours of adjacent objects, or those distant from it. The difference in colour on bright and dull days is enormous.

In order to promote health pure bright colours should not be used in masses in home decoration as they are much too crude and jarring. In bed and sitting rooms subdued shades are best; in bedrooms lavender and similar shades; in sitting rooms shades with a warmer touch, such as rose or pale yellow, or mixtures of both. Cold colours should not be used in rooms with a chilly northern aspect. Gold, straw and citron tend to raise the spirits.

Do not use yellow, orange, red or black in bedrooms, as the first three tend to keep one awake, and black is a depressing colour.

In dining rooms, colours which stimulate both appetite and conversation should be used, such as rose tints, a little crimson, yellow or gold, or a judicious combination of all.

Chromotherapy does not *cure* disease. *Nature* alone can do that. The right use of colour, however, assists Nature. The body has a wonderful self-adjusting mechanism, and if attention is paid to diet, hygiene, rest, sleep and thought, the right colours will accelerate the process. Colours do not produce the coarse vibrations generated by drugs and chemicals. Vibrations produced by sunshine, light and colour are of the subtlest nature.

All the colours of the spectrum are used, often through filters, and sometimes combined with other colours to produce shades and tints. The main centres for treatment are the nape of the neck, the entire spine, solar plexus, chest, abdomen and lumbar region. Colour is applied locally for specific ailments such as catarrh, rheumatism, eye troubles and constipation, and astounding results can be achieved at the hands of a skilled practitioner.

THE APPLICATION OF COLOURS

Colours may be applied in two ways: by general diffusion and by local concentration. The first consists of focusing light rays on the body, concentrating on the back, where the vibrations recharge tired cells and renew their vitality. The patient sits or lies in a relaxed position and is bathed in light for thirty minutes. Should treatment be extended for a longer period it is always carried out in a lying position.

In the second method light is focused on the affected area, different light filters being used to rectify different conditions, and exposure is generally for fifteen to twenty minutes, followed by general diffusion for half an hour.

Light and colour penetrate the skin in the same way as sunlight and have a direct action on the protoplasm. Exactly how this happens is not known. We know, however, that certain cosmic rays have a greater power of penetration than light. Some scientists think that penetration of the body cells is achieved by osmosis (Greek, *osmos*, pushing) which pushes light and colour vibrations through the membranes, and these are accepted by sympathetic areas of the body.

Students of yoga and of the Chinese Canon of Health (*Hei Ching*) know that the first harmony of the body is achieved by the equilibrium between *ida* and *pingala* (in yoga) and *yang* and *yin* (in *Hei Ching*). It is on this principle that acupuncture is based.

Vibrations of light and colour create harmonious vibrations of etheric matter, recharging and vitalizing the organism. If the particles within the body are nonconductive, have a different rate of vibration, or if the incoming light vibrations are too powerful for the normal resistance of the body, an abnormal reaction may be produced and much harm done, as happens when ultraviolet rays are directed on to the skin for more than three minutes, or on to the eyes, which are delicate structures; or if strong sunlight plays on the skin for any length of time. Because of these factors the conditions of an ailing body and its reactions to certain colours must be studied and understood.

Ultra-Blue-Violet Range
The conditions which respond to these colours are haemorrhage, inflammation, tuberculosis, excessive menstruation, diarrhoea, excitable conditions, palpitation, insomnia and spinal irritation. Hector Durville says that bees reared under violet light produce more honey and of a higher quality than those reared under white light.

Red
Red light has been used with success for spastic conditions,

congestion, anaemia, poor digestion, muscular pain, ear-ache, tuberculosis, deficient menstruation and chills.

Yellow and orange

Yellow and orange light are used to treat cerebral lassitude, nervous debility, feeble nerve action, tumours, hard congestion, sluggish liver, weak kidneys, despondency and exhaustion.

Dr Podolsky says: 'The world is full of colours and each one exerts a very definite effect on our mind and psyche.' One American football coach believed so firmly in this theory that he had two rooms specially painted: one in bright red in which he delivered pep talks to stimulate his team before games; the other in blue for rest and recuperation. His team was outstandingly successful.

COLOUR ENGINEERING

In America, colour engineers are highly paid specialists who vie in importance with the leaders of other professions. Some specialize in healing; others act as consultants to commercial and industrial corporations. In the field of advertising, for instance, they have found that certain colours on the covers of books sell better than others, so that red and yellow and combinations of both are preferred by the public to blue, purple, violet and dark green.

They have proved that the public has an aversion to blue and purple foods, with the exceptions of jams, preserves, beetroot, grapes and berries. This may seem irrational; perhaps all human likes and dislikes appear irrational until one realizes how colour vibrations act. That is why so much food is dyed to give it 'eye appeal', and provided the dyes are harmless, such as anatto which is used to colour certain cheeses, or have some nutritional value, their use is permissible.

Soda, which is put into water when boiling peas 'to bring out their colour', is harmful, for not only does it destroy vitamin C but it interferes with digestion.

AN EXPERIMENT WITH COLOURS

Years ago Samuel G. Hibben, a colour engineer in Chicago, undertook an experiment in the course of which he invited a number of friends to dinner at a leading hotel in the city. Only the choicest foods and wines were served. Unknown to his guests Hibben had the room illuminated by special filters which eliminated all the colours except green and red. The celery turned pink, steaks looked a whitish-grey, milk turned to blood-red, salads seemed blue, peas and oysters were jet-black, and a bowl of peanuts looked crimson. One after another the guests were affected. Some lost their appetites and a few felt queasy. Quickly normal lighting was restored and immediately the guests recovered both appetite and health. This proved to Hibben that colours affect not only sight but taste and smell.

HOWARD KETCHAM

Howard Ketcham, the well-known colour engineer, was once approached by a prominent society hostess who explained: 'I am giving an important dinner party and would like to make the occasion as exciting as possible. Do you think colours would help?'

Ketcham was sure they would. He installed a number of 1000-watt lamps, placed magenta slides over them and focused them on the floor and furniture. Then he switched off all other lights so that the room was suffuced with a soft, relaxing magenta glow, and when the diners sat down their minds were relieved of worry and anxiety and the event proved to be the most successful dinner that season. Ketcham said: 'Without any other help those magenta lamps were the equivalent of two to three cocktails before dinner.'

PURPLE – THE ROYAL COLOUR

Though purple is the royal colour it should be used with circumspection in house decoration. One Harley Street specialist realized that a wealthy patient consulted him because she was unbearably depressed, for which there seemed no reason. On looking up her history he found that she was always much better after returning from holiday, so decided that there must be something in her home which caused depression. He made an appointment to visit her at home, and when the butler let him in he was appalled to find that every square inch of wallpaper and the flowers and decorations were in shades of purple, deep violet and heliotrope, whose effect was unbearably gloomy.

He advised her to take a world cruise and allow a colour expert to have the house redecorated in her absence. This was done in yellow and light greens, and when weeks after her return she visited him again he found a singularly cheerful patient, abounding in vitality. Never again did she suffer from depression.

BLACK MAY CAUSE SUICIDE

It is not without reason that the clothing and trapping of undertakers are black, for the intention is to produce solemnity and draw attention to the sadness of the occasion. When Blackfriars Bridge in London was painted black, a colour which seemed to attract the helpless and the hopeless, many people committed suicide by leaping off it. Eventually public clamour was such that the LCC had it painted green.

THE ABSORBING POWER OF BLACK

No colour absorbs as much heat as black. Extensive experiments have proved that black central-heating radiators absorb more, but reflect less heat than those painted white or aluminium.

For more than fifty years scientists have heated water tanks in homes and run engines in the tropics by solar heat. In some instances aluminium radiators are used to reflect sunlight, and in temperate zones they are painted black to absorb it. After experiments with various colours Dr Cleland McVeigh, head of the Department of Mechanical and Production Engineering, Brighton Polytechnic, used a black radiator on the roof of the building to convert solar energy into hot water because he found it more efficient than any other colour.

For most of the wet summer of 1975 the water in his 30-gallon collector tanks reached 60°C (150°F), and even in mid-December and in January the temperature touched 40°C (112°F) at the end of the day, which is warm enough for a bath.

Britain wastes an enormous amount of heat (and money) by ignoring solar heat, but steps are being taken to rectify this and new homes, offices and even factories are being designed with water tanks on the roofs, which are covered by black glass or aluminium to absorb the rays of the sun which, though most of us do not realize it, throws off some heat even on cold, cloudy days.

The heads of commercial and industrial houses would do well to consult colour experts. If they did, efficiency would increase. When on the advice of one a London concern changed its factory wallpaper from grey to cream and rose, absenteeism from minor ailments such as headaches and stomach upsets fell by about 10 per cent, and in their offices typing speeds went up by 12 per cent and shorthand speeds by 20 per cent, and fewer errors were made.

PROFESSOR PICCARD

It is true to speak of colours being warm and cold. In 1921 Professor Auguste Piccard painted black the gondola of the balloon in which he intended to explore the stratosphere to ensure that he and his crew would remain comfortably warm when they were thousands of feet above the clouds. But when he got there he wished he had not, for though the temperature outside was $-75°F$, he and his crew sweltered in 100 degrees of heat!

For his next flight he had the gondola painted white, whereupon the temperature at high altitudes fell to 28°F.

LOSSES DUE TO EVAPORATION

In the 1920's an oil company in Texas found that evaporation from storage tanks was so great that it was making a hole in the profits. So they called in a colour engineer, who selected four 12,000-gallon tanks and said: 'Paint one black, one red, one grey and one white.' After four and a half months the levels were checked and it was found that 1000 gallons were missing from the black tank, 257 from the red, 150 from the grey, and only 50 from the white. That was convincing enough for all the tanks to be painted white.

Tests were then made on 55,000-barrel crude oil tanks, and over a period of twelve months it was found that evaporation in tanks painted black exceeded by 200 barrels that in tanks painted aluminium.

WHITE PAINT BEST FOR TROPICS

Men have always dressed in white in the tropics because they felt that white was the coolest colour. Now it has been proved that it is. In 1933 the Canadian National Steamship Co. carried out tests by painting white all their ships in tropical waters. The first of the line was the SS *Prince David* on the Miami-Nassau run, and it was found that the temperature in the interior of the ship fell by no less than 15 per cent.

When the result of this experiment was published the White Star Line had the hull of the *Mauretania*, then in dry dock after a tropical cruise, painted white, with the result that the temperature in the interior fell more than 10°F on her next voyage. Today all banana boats plying between the West Indies and Britain are painted white.

Shipowners in the Yukon learnt about these experiments and decided to find out whether colours would help them to hasten the thaw in spring. Of the various dyes tried, the most effective and cheapest proved to be lamp-black, so a wide path of lamp-black mixed with oil was spread over the ice along the route ships would follow, the oil being used to prevent the ice freezing at night. Each day as the sun's rays increased in power they burrowed into the black strip, melted the snow far more rapidly than that on either side, and enabled ships to pass into the sea days before it would have been possible otherwise, saving the company hundreds of thousands of dollars.

BLACK ABSORBS HEAT: WHITE REFLECTS IT

More than any other nation, the Russians have experimented with colours in their Arctic towns. North of the 70th parallel on Dixon Island, walls during summer absorb twice as much radiation heat as in Crimean resorts, so they painted the walls of houses white and have found that the *reflected radiation*, which is as much as 4°C, has the effect of keeping the *streets* much warmer. The interiors of homes and factories are heated by oil or electricity.

ABSORBENT PROPERTIES OF COLOURS

The Russians have also experimented with colours to absorb noise, for they have found that certain colours absorb and deaden noise vibrations. Scientists have compiled tables giving the best noise-muffling colours. Light green and light blue have proved most effective in damping high-pitched sounds, and by painting the walls of homes and factories in these colours the effects of noise was reduced by several decibels. Further experiments are being carried out and when these are complete people who are pestered by their neighbour's radio, the high-pitched scream of jets and noises produced by tube trains and cars a few feet from their homes will be able to get some measure of relief. A reduction of even a few decibels may make all the difference between a normal life and existence in a Bedlam.

COLOURS HELP TO CURE PARALYTIC CHILDREN

In 1937 when an epidemic of infantile paralysis raged in Teignmouth, the disease was halted by the advice of the Australian, Nurse Kenny, who has achieved miracles fighting this infection. She had the rooms of patients painted blue, and nurses were dressed in red capes and blue smocks – bright colours which stimulated the victims and changed their outlook. She also coupled chromotherapy with brine baths and general hydrotherapy, with such remarkable results that her methods were adopted by several cottage hospitals. Scores of children stricken by polio soon started to show signs of recovery and many regained health completely.

COLOUR AND MUSIC

Since the earliest times colour and music have been associated. The Egyptians, Chaldeans, Chinese, Hindus and Greeks wore garments of certain colours and played certain types of music during religious ceremonies or on state occasions. With them the link was probably instinctive or inspirational. Not till the eighteenth century did Father Castel, a Jesuit priest, invent his 'ocular keyboard'. This he did by assuming that the seven colours of the spectrum corresponded to the seven tones of the musical scale.

In his system C was represented by blue; C sharp by willow green; D by light green; E by yellow; F by saffron; F sharp by orange; G by red; G sharp by crimson; A by violet; A sharp by violet-blue; B by spectral blue. He then repeated the octave, the colours growing progressively paler with each repetition. He also used music with colours to soothe, stimulate and excite.

Others have applied their minds to the same idea. In his Theory of Colours Goethe said that Leonard Hoffman published a book in 1786 in which colours were associated with musical instruments, the sound of the violoncello being indigo blue, the violin ultramarine, the horn scarlet, and so on. In 1812 Dr G. T. L. Sachs, a Bavarian albino, wrote a thesis in which he described his experiences in 'hearing' various colours. He went even further and linked colours with vowels and consonants, notes of the musical scale, the sounds produced by various instruments, the names of towns, days of the week, dates, historical periods, phases of human existence and all sorts of other events. To Sachs the vowel A was vermilion, E pink, I white, O red, Ou Black, and U white. The consonant D was yellow, M white, S dark blue, etc, till each letter was endowed with a colour or combinations of colours.

Unlike normal people the blind have to imagine not only the shapes of objects but events and sounds. A writer in 1834 said that when a man blind from birth was asked what he thought the colour red was like, he replied without hesitation: 'It must be very like the sound of a trumpet!' This approximated to Dr Sachs' scarlet horn.

COLOUR, ART AND POETRY

Many famous men have associated colours with various activities. Leonardo da Vinci said, for instance, that violet was the best colour for concentration.

Many artists and musicians associate colour with music. Van Gogh was so convinced of the reality of 'colour hearing' that he tried to learn to play the piano in order to improve his sense of colour, but as he insisted on equating certain notes with Prussian blue, emerald green and chrome yellow, his instructor, who lacked Van Gogh's imagination, said he was mad and refused to continue his lessons.

A number of poets have associated colours with music too. Swinburne spoke of 'invisible sound', and Blake, Keats, Shelley and Edgar Allan Poe compared sound with colour. So did the French writers Maupassant, Baudelaire and Rimbaud. In a lyrical passage one poet invited his sweetheart to ride with him 'in a cab as green as the music of the oboe'.

Another said that words like *France, espérance* and *ange* had an aristocratic air and appeared in colour, but words containing *ou* appeared dingy and hang-dog.

CHROMOAESTHESIA

When objects are associated with colours the condition is known as *chromoaesthesia*. Some say that the German language sounds green, English brown, Greek yellow and French blue. They also have grey headaches, blue toothaches and green rheumatism. Such association requires a degree of imagination such as is inherent in musicians, poets and perhaps writers, but is not often found in prosaic, humdrum folk like civil servants and factory workers.

OCULAR KEYBOARDS

Father Castel has had many disciples throughout the years. In 1927 a Russian named Theremin gave an unusual recital at the Opera in Paris where at the end of the performance the theatre was darkened and a shaft of light was focused on him. As he continued to play the lighting was changed to conform to the mood of his music. His method became extremely popular and there were many imitators, especially in cinemas where Wurlitzer organs were installed.

Others, among them Scriabin and Schönberg, have written

music intended to be played with changing lights, and in 1922 Sir Arthur Bliss composed a symphony in which each movement was labelled with the name of a different colour. Shortly before his death Scriabin started a work which was never finished, in which music was to be accompanied by gestures, colours and perfumes.

Most great musicians have associated music with colour. Scriabin first got his ideas of association when he stayed with Rimsky-Korsakoff and they played a piece in D major. 'A very golden key,' he remarked and Rimsky-Korsakoff concurred. But later when Scriabin professed his liking for the key of F-sharp major and added: 'I like the violet tones,' there was disagreement.

'Violet!' thundered Rimsky-Korsakoff. 'Are you blind? The key in F-sharp is bright green.'

Neither realized that the salient characteristic in chromoaesthesia is that few people agree exactly about the colours they see. Beethoven said that B-minor was the black key; Rimsky-Korsakoff that sunlight is C-major, F-sharp strawberry red, and the cold colours all minor.

HERMAN DAREWESKI

Herman Dareweski, composer and concert pianist, carried out a number of experiments with music and colour and said that a piece he had written in a friend's garden in bright sunshine could not possibly have been composed by him in a drab and sombre London fog. Colours had a significant effect on his output. Rich orange brought back the past vividly. Blue and mauve depressed. Tango red and yellow exhilarated. Scarlet irritated. Pale amber fired his imagination. Pink made him fanciful and purple doleful. His music was draped in colours to produce corresponding moods. Normal people lack his degree of sensitivity.

Dareweski tabulated colours with his various moods and found this a great help to acquiring the appropriate mood for composing. When asked to write a piece of music round a Russian snow scene he found it difficult to start but eventually induced the right mood of desolation, vastness, extreme cold and the jingle of sleigh bells by gazing for a time through a strip of blue gelatine.

LADY MURIEL ANDERSON

In 1952 Lady Muriel Anderson held an exhibition of her pictures at Foyle's Art Gallery, which were inspired by music and colour. Not everyone could understand them, so she had to explain. 'I have psychic powers. I paint by tapping the Thought Ray, which is just as real as a radio wave.' This process enabled her to translate music into visual form. One of her pictures, *Rhapsody in Blue*, has a white motif on a black background; another, *Symphony Orchestra*, consists of a series of concentric circles of different colours to show all the instruments striking the same note. Her painting *Sun King*, created from music and movement, depicts a ballet.

ALEXANDER CANNON

Dr Alexander Cannon, psychiatrist and research scientist at the Colney Hatch Mental Hospital in the 1930s, had considerable success in calming obstreperous inmates by the use of coloured lights. He specialized in therapeutic mind control and on one occasion conducted an experiment in sleep in a public hall in which 4000 people took part. At the start the stage was flooded with red light, then two green lights were focused through thin black curtains while at the back of the stage an orchestra played 'My Heart Is Sleeping'.

Cannon stood behind the curtain and sent out suggestions which made the audience drowsy. Within thirty *seconds* about half of them were asleep and within a minute or two most of the others dropped off! On waking all said they felt more refreshed than they had been for months.

'I am looking forward to the time,' said Cannon, 'when the

BBC will give its half hour of slumber music with appropriate colour combinations by television.' Colour television was then a long way off, but since his day nothing has been done to put his ideas into practice, though the number of insomniacs who resort to sleeping drugs must have increased by millions.

In the course of his experiments Cannon found that colour can alter a man's disposition, make him change his career, cure him of some diseases and, by preventing forgetfulness, enable him to avoid accidents! This last alone is worth knowing.

He proved during his sojourn at Colney Hatch that those who live in rooms decorated mainly in red grow quarrelsome; if the motif is grass-green they become amiable; and in rose-golden rooms they tend to be affectionate. He found that appetite, energy and the mind were affected by colour, which also influences the functions of the body through the glands.

He said that from his experience he found that generally speaking red stimulates, purple heals, orange raises the spirits, blue soothes, green pleases and brown is restful. Grey is bound up by fear and those assailed by fears should wear rich blue or golden brown, whichever suits their colouring best.

Mr J. Sturzaker, radiesthesist and chromotherapist, says that the choice of a shade which vibrates in harmony with a patient's vibrations is of the utmost importance in healing.

Little by little experiments and the results of experience have added to our fund of knowledge about colour and its effects on people. Mr G. A. Bowler of Leicester, a registered nurse and chromotherapist, has made plants grow four times their normal rate by focusing infrared rays on them, which he says are also very effective in the treatment of boils, earache, bronchitis, muscular pains and other ailments, especially when used in conjunction with music. He has found that the concentration of blue light together with relaxing music will often terminate pain in twenty minutes. The note G, for instance, which has 45 vibrations a second and relates to blue, used in conjunction with Debussy's 'Clair de Lune' has cured many a pain.

COLOUR AND THE EYES

William Luftig, MD (Berlin), believed that eye diseases could be cured without resorting to the knife. To cure disease, he argued, the fundamental cause should be eliminated.

> The eye does not require any surgical operation if one acts according to the causal relationship between the eye and the body and combines the local treatment with a treatment of the disease cause and the bodily constitution . . .

> The eye is not a self-contained unit and not independent of the rest of the organism. The eye disease is in the majority of cases nothing but a local manifestation of a general disease. This means that each treatment consists of two parts: the constitutional therapy which puts the body in its entirety into proper working order, and the application of local measures, which have a beneficial effect on the eye.

> Every surgeon believes surgery to be the ideal method of treating eye diseases. Practical experience has shown, however, that we must treat the ill person and not merely the disease product in the eye. Local treatment can never be the appropriate remedy for a complaint which involves the whole organism. Operations mean a mutilation of the eye for life and achieve no *healing* results.

> A therapy which wishes to secure a completely successful result must combine local light-therapeutic measures with electro-and hydrotherapy, relaxation, physical culture and detoxication. *

Luftig first regulated the diet of his patients to ensure that every organ was getting its proper quota of nutrients. Light treatment was then applied. This he found, in an experience extending over twenty-five years, acted as a foundation in the treatment of organic and functional disorders in all parts of the eyeball. Red, blue, green and yellow were the principal colours used for light baths to the head.

* *How to Cure Eye Diseases Without Operation* (Luftig, 1939).

Red light: Luftig found that red light has a stimulating influence on both blood and nerves; it excites the circulation to vigorous motion; causes hyperaemia. It is therefore contra-indicated in cases of fresh inflammation such as acute retinitis and iritis.

Red light is invaluable in treating cataract and detachment of the retina, where it increases blood and lymph current and initiates and supports the removal of deposits between the lens fibres in cataract and of the fluid accumulation under the retina in retinal detachment. Under no conditions should red light be used in acute inflammatory conditions, which call for the cooling action of blue.

Luftig had known cases of paralysed eye muscle to be stirred into activity by red light waves.

Blue light: should be used in cases of inflammation, for nervous symptoms of the eye and for attacks of pain, as in cases of anaemia or lack of blood in the eye. Blue counteracts inflammation, stops the rush of blood to the head and eyes and, if the eyelids are swollen, helps to reduce heat and swelling of tissue. Blue, which has marked pain-relieving properties, will relieve neuralgic pains in head and eyes. When pain is severe, as in glaucoma for instance, blue in connection with concentrated white light reduces pressure and alleviates pain.

Green light: stands halfway between blue and red. It is less active and positive than red, and less passive and negative than blue. It is never contra-indicated in eye diseases, stimulates mildly and is of value in any state of the eyes, and it is fortunate that green is so profuse in Nature. A sojourn in the country, where there is so much green, always rests the eyes and helps eye sufferers.

Green also has a distinct regulative action on blood circulation and these characteristics make it an important therapeutic agent in all eye diseases. It has the power to prevent the decay of eye tissue and the growth of disease germs, and in cases of iris inflammation disperses the formation of pus in the anterior eye chamber.

Yellow light: is very warm, stimulates the nerves and is effective where the eye muscles are paralysed. Yellow increases and intensifies the distribution of the blood and lymph current in the eyes and is often used for glaucoma, cataract and detachment of the retina, as it stimulates and increases the fluid stream in the eyeball.

In cataract the increased speed of circulation enables the fluids to carry away particles of deposits in the opaque lens; in glaucoma it removes irritating substances from the tissues of the eye; and in retinal detachment the increased circulation promotes the absorption of liquids accumulated under the detached retina. Yellow is of special value in chronic eye diseases, as it livens sluggish sections of the eyeball and transforms the passive and unresponsive parts into activity.

Luftig used the following colour combinations with considerable success:

Glaucoma: yellow and green.

Cataract: red and yellow.

Retinal detachment: alternately, one day blue and the next red, both in combination with concentrated white light.

Retinitis: blue to start, then strong white light, finally green.

Conjunctivitis and iritis: blue and white.

Purulent iritis: green and blue.

Squint: green and concentrated white light, alternating with blue and white.

Paralysis of the intrinsic eye muscles: red and yellow.

Luftig always emphasized that colour healing was only part of the curative measures employed by him, and would have comparatively little effect if the diet of the patient was not reformed and regulated and the condition of the blood stream balanced. Only then would the eye respond fully.

5
The Power of Music

The *Oxford English Dictionary* gives one of the definitions of music as: 'Sounds in melodic or harmonious combination, whether produced by voice or instruments.' The physical laws which apply to other sounds apply also to music which, generally speaking, is pleasant, though tastes differ widely and what is pleasing to one may be torture to another.

The appeal of music is to the emotions, not the intellect, for some of the best brains had no ear for music and neither vocal nor instrumental music gave them the slightest pleasure. Among those unfortunates were Hume the philosopher, Dr Johnson, Sir Walter Scott, Sir Robert Peel and Lord Byron, and it gave the poet Samuel Rogers actual discomfort.

Since the dawn of civilization music has been used to influence men's minds and spirits and through them their bodies. The Chinese, Hindus, Egyptians, Babylonians, Greeks and Arabs all used music to soothe and heal. We know that more than a thousand years before the birth of Christ 'David took a harp and played with his hand; so Saul was refreshed and was well, and the evil spirit departed from him.' (1 Samuel 16. 23.)

The Jews were, and always have been, musicians of great skill and virtuosity and the Bible names more than a dozen string, wind and percussion instruments: harp, lute, sackbut, viol, cornet, dulcimer, organ, pipe, trumpet, bells, cymbals, shawm, tabret and timbrel.

Solomon's Temple had an orchestra of wind instruments, a male choir in which each member had a minimum of five years' training, and a boys' choir to supplement it and add sweetness to the singing.

ANCIENT INDIA

In Ancient India great stress was placed upon both the healing and the destructive power of music. They said: 'Ideas precede words; and words can be creative. The sounds made by humans can carry an influence of mind over matter.' They urged men to study words and sentences and produce the forms of speech known as mantras which have a material effect upon the mind, emotions and body, and even upon inanimate objects!

Indian music seems meaningless to many in the West and we are only beginning to study and appreciate it. To our ears Chinese and Japanese music seem even more discordant and tuneless, but some of us are now beginning to understand it. Tastes in music vary widely. Many enjoy music only if it has melody, rhythm and swing, which those with 'educated' tastes label as sugary. The advanced revel in Bartok, Honegger, Scriabin and Stravinsky, mainly beacause of their technique. Teenagers prefer noisy music with a hypnotic beat. Each kind of music may have either a therapeutic or a destructive effect, depending on the audience and the emotions aroused.

According to Indian mythology their music is a divine art and a gift of the gods. Their first musicians were supposed to have been the eternal trinity: Brahma, Vishnu and Shiva. Shiva worked out the infinite modes of rhythm; Brahma the time-beat; Krishna, the incarnation of Vishnu, invented the flute; and Saraswati, Goddess of Wisdom, the veena, earliest of string instruments.

The ragas, or fixed melodic scales, form the foundation of

Hindu music, and the six basic ragas have 126 derivatives called *raginis* (wives) and *putras* (sons). Each raga has a minimum of five notes and corresponds to an hour of the day, a season of the year, or a presiding deity. The theory seems much too complicated for most Western minds. The rishis (sages) realized that Man and Nature are one and AUM or OM is the primitive sound by which Man can control all natural manifestations by the use of mantras.

BHARATA, FATHER OF INDIAN MUSIC

Bharata, the real founder of Indian music, laid down 129 talas or time measures and is said to have isolated 32 kinds of tala in the song of the lark. The tala is based on human movements: the double time of walking, the triple time of respiration during sleep, when inhalation is twice the time of exhalation. He recognized that the human voice is the most perfect instrument of sound, so Hindu music confines itself to the voice range of three octaves and for this reason melody rather than harmony is stressed.

THE MOGHUL ERA

When early in the sixteenth century the Moghuls established their empire in Hindustan they did their utmost to eliminate every vestige of native culture except music. Their most famous emperor, Akbar the Great, who exercised a remarkable degree of tolerance, actually encouraged it. He summoned Miyan Tan Sen, the court musician, and commanded him to sing a night raga when the sun was in its zenith, but no sooner did the singer intone the requisite mantra than the entire palace and its environs were enveloped in darkness.

On another occasion Akbar commanded a musician who had mastered the Deepaka Raga (played only during summer evenings to arouse compassion) to perform for his benefit.

The singer knew he could not do so at the wrong time without awakening supernatural forces, so took the precaution of standing up to his neck in the sacred Jumna (a tributary of the Ganges). No sooner had he worked up into a crescendo than his crystal-pure notes heated the atmosphere, which vibrated so fiercely that the water boiled. 'Sing on!' roared Akbar and within seconds the air burst into flame and the singer was consumed.

We know that scientists can make chips of wood burst into flames and cook food if the right vibrations are produced. Why should the human voice not be able to produce them? The quality or timbre of musical instruments – that is, the vibrations – depends on their resonators, which in the organ for instance depends on the resonance of the column of air in the pipes. In the violin the resonators are the bridge, the ribs and the belly of the instrument, its shape and even the varnish and care bestowed in the making. The human voice also has its resonators: the mouth, nasal and head cavities, and the breast bone, and the richness of tone (or lack of it) depends on the training, skill and natural gifts of the singer. Apparently singers in ancient India knew how to develop these to the full.

DOROTHY ABAYAKOON

Dorothy Abayakoon, graduate of the Art Training School, Melbourne, was art illustrator to the United States Educational Foundation (Ceylon), where she worked for the leading newspapers. There she established her own art school before coming to London. Music (piano and harp) is one of her hobbies, and she trained at the Royal College of Music and the Trinity College of Music, and composes her own lyrics and sets them to music.

She has done research into Dravidian (Sumerian) music which was taken to Western India by Abraham Pundit (Al-Brahmin), a priest of Brahma (God) – hence the name Abraham, leader of the Hebrews. The Indian harp, a favourite instrument of the Hindus, was played at King Solomon's court (*c*.1000 BC) to dissipate stress and pressures. It is from this instrument that the piano was developed, for the piano holds the harp in its structure.

Long before – about 10,000 BC – the Arayans and Dravidians of the Indian sub-continent, which then included Persia and the Tigris-Euphrates basins of the Aryan Mittani tribes, developed several instruments, of which the lyre, lute, psaltery and harp were modifications, and their sounds were modified as *Sa – Ri – Ga – Ma – Pa – Da – Ni – Sah*, the first and last 180 degrees apart, i.e. at the extreme ends of the scale.

As according to their knowledge all music was related to the life-force emanating from a Celestial Source, the sound OM has to be transmitted in a proper manner. In the West only the Roman Catholic Church has preserved the divine powers in the priests' chants, using words like *OM-nium* and *OM-nis* to represent Brahman, the *OM-nipotent*.

Dorothy Abayakoon has composed piano music for the twelve signs of the zodiac to interpret the meaning of each sign. This has been released through the piano and recorded, coupled with *mantra-intonations* giving the correct benefic vibrations for the twelve signs, individually and collectively.

MEDICINE AND MUSIC

The best musicians have always been alive to the power of music. In ancient Greece Apollo, God of Music, was also God of Medicine. Hippocrates took patients to the temple to listen to music and Plato and Aristotle spoke and wrote about its healing effects on mind and body. 'Melody, rhythm, gesture and words were all consciously adapted to the production of a single precisely conceived emotional effect; the listener was in a position clearly to understand and appraise the value of the mood excited in him; instead of being exhausted and confused by a chaos of vague and conflicting emotion he had the sense of relief which accompanies the deliverance of a definite passion, and returned to his ordinary business "purged", as they said, and tranquillized, by a process which he understood, directed to an end of which he approved.'*

Plato said: 'Musical training is a more potent instrument than any other because rhythm and harmony find their way into the inward places of the soul, on which they mightily fasten, imparting grace and making him who is rightly educated graceful. The introduction of a new kind of music must be shunned as imperilling the whole stage since styles of music are never disturbed without affecting the most important political institutions. It is the essence of order and leads to all that is good and just and beautiful.'

With this one may not necessarily agree.

HYPNOTIC EFFECTS OF MUSICS

The Indian musician picks on one particular melody and develops it *ad infinitum*, which palls on most Western ears and seems monotonous. Ravel did much the same in *Bolero*, which he composed because he was wagered he could not write a piece which developed the same theme and lasted twenty minutes. When first played in public it drove one woman in the audience into hysterics. Some psychiatrists have recommended *Bolero*, played softly, to patients who could not sleep, for they found that halfway through the long-playing record they were lulled into unconsciousness.

ANTIPATHETIC MUSIC

There is no accounting for musical tastes. All types of music do not appeal to all types of people. Where music is concerned individuals are extremely selective, if not actually conservative. Music which makes a woman almost swoon and drool with pleasure may cause her husband to go berserk, and many a marriage has foundered on musical shoals. Teenagers, who love noise and have an excess of energy, indulge in pop

* Lowes Dickenson, *The Greek View of Life* (Methuen, 1896).

and beat, together with the antics which accompany them, and send parents into paroxysms of rage, which lead youngsters into complaining: 'No one understands us.'

Listeners do not take kindly to the new or the novel, and when Alfredo Casella first tried to interest audiences in the works of Stravinsky and Honegger, which are now accepted by all, he was pelted with tomatoes! Even Johann Strauss was cried down when he attempted to popularize the kind of music associated with his name. As for the dance which went with it – people said it was the height of vulgarity, but today nothing seems more innocuous.

This has happened ever since Man first made music. A Greek historian tells us that when Timotheus played the lyre in the Phrygian mode to Alexander the Great, the general threw himself into a violent temper and calmed down only when the musician changed to the Lydian mode. One has only to listen to 'Desert Island Discs' or 'Housewives' Choice' on radio to realize that what is ineffable bliss to one may be sheer hell to another. Such is the power of music.

My idea of purgatory would be to work in an office or factory where music is piped throughout the day for the benefit (?) of the employees. Why they do not go mad is a mystery, but apparently most of them are unaffected and actually enjoy it. Music which one dislikes or does not wish to hear can be a form of refined torture and an assault on the individual, and one of the sanest laws of the land is that which makes it illegal to submit all and sundry to vibratory poison churned out from transistor radios in trains, buses, and in public places, and forbids householders from playing music so loudly that neighbours are inconvenienced.

Baudelaire once said: 'I love Wagner but the music I prefer is that of a cat hung up by its tail outside a window trying to stick to the panes of glass, which I find at the same time strange, irritating and singularly harmonious.' Few in Britain would agree, even if they could bring themselves to countenance such cruelty, for the sound would curdle the blood of most people.

MEDICAL USES OF MUSIC

'I should like to inquire,' wrote Frances M. Banks to *The Guardian*, 'whether ordinary hospitals have ever organized research on the therapeutic value of music, and whether the virtues of classical music outweigh those of jazz as an aid to recovery.

'A recent week in hospital prompts this inquiry. A minor operation, skillfully performed, excellent nursing in happy surroundings provided a week of blissful rest – or would have done but for the accompaniment of the "Light" – the assault and battery of jazz on the ear. This was not so much the fault of authority as of the patients, who clearly wanted it – most of them. But ought they to have it? If what you fancy musically is not good (as staple diet), does it do you good?'

Since that letter was written patients in hospitals are equipped with individual earphones and can select from a number of programmes without offending others in the same ward.

THE ANCIENT EGYPTIANS

The ancient Egyptians, whose medicine was based on that of the Assyrians and Babylonians, used music to cure as long ago as 1600BC, and in 287BC Theophrastus, a Greek who studied their methods, stated that flute music was played to sufferers from sciatica, rheumatism and other pains which drugs failed to heal, and for the stings of insects. In the cool of the evening rulers and high officials would glide down the Nile in their barges and relax from the strains and stresses of official duties to the music of the lute and the harp.

For thousands of years the right sort of music has always made men feel better, for if the spirits are raised health almost invariably improves. The Hindus have always believed that music and colour were aids to well-being. This is true of all civilized peoples, and we now know that the ancient Druids were much concerned with harmonics and music.

COURT MUSICIANS

With the spread of culture in Europe, monarchs established their own orchestras and appointed musicians to play music to suit their moods. Philip v of Spain, who suffered badly from melancholia, was cured by Farinelli, one of the finest musicians in the country. Today he would be treated by a psychiatrist.

THE TARANTELLA

Julius Hecker said in *The Epidemics of The Middle Ages* (now out of print) that between the tenth and fourteenth centuries the Germans were affected by a 'dancing mania' which convulsed the body. The disease spread rapidly and did not die out for two centuries. The victims danced, leapt, twitched and screamed and eventually fell exhausted. The only way to combat tarantulism was by music, which started at a brisk tempo in keeping with the movements of the victims and then slowed to lull them to sleep.

When the affliction spread to Italy physicians there said that it was caused by the bite of the dreaded tarantula spider and they called the disease St Vitus's Dance whereas, in fact, it was chorea, which attacks children usually at the age of puberty and prevents them from controlling their limbs. Giorgio Baglivi, the greatest physician of his time, who was also an accomplished musician, obtained gratifying results by treating patients with gay, lively melodies. He formed 'medical orchestras', organized 'therapeutical tours' throughout the country, and eventually the disease was conquered.

Many instruments were used in the cure of St Vitus's Dance: harp, violin, clarinet, flute and the French bagpipe. The flute was the most popular as it could be carried easily, and Pepys, who had a passion for it, retails a story by a traveller from Italy, who said: 'There are fiddlers to go up and down the country, in the fields and everywhere, in expectation of being hired by those who are stung.' The tarantella, now a dance in 6–8 time, has evolved from those old tunes.

By the sixteenth century musicians had begun to realize that music had therapeutic value and in 1548 the Faculty of Medicine in Paris set for public discussion a subject on the theme: *An musica Medico sit tenanda*? (Is music to be borne in mind by the physician?).

COGAN AND BROWNE

Thomas Cogan (1545–1607), physician and herbalist, was one of the first in Europe to use music to heal the sick. 'I counsel all students,' he wrote, 'often times to refresh their wearied minds with some sort of melody. For so they should drive away the dumps of melancholy, and make their spirits more lively to learn.' He urged all his patients to listen to music and play it if they could.

Richard Browne (1625–94), also a famous doctor, who wrote *Medicina Musica*, stated: 'That singing is an enemy to melancholy thoughts, and a pleasing promoter of mirth and joy, is what we find by daily experience . . . by singing the soul should be delightfully ravished, and filled with gay and enlivening ideas . . . by raising the discernment of the ear into delicacy, every fine tremulous oscillation, which to vulgar ears would be imperceptible, and thereby much of the harmony be abated, is distinctly felt and enjoyed; this pleasure may also be improved in some measure by habituating ourselves to sing; for by exercise the organs will gain a greater strength and agility in their action, and thereby be adapted more quickly to modulate the voice into tune.'

A doctor who might easily have become a musician was Claver Morris (1657–1727), who founded the Musick-Club in Wells, for he was an orchestra in himself, singing and performing expertly on the violin, organ, harpsichord, double bass, flute, oboe and bassoon. He even found time to improve some of these instruments; and wherever he went he was resounding in his praise of music as an aid to health.

Gradually the idea that music, whether played or sung, is good for health, gathered force and in 1744 John Armstrong, a leading physician, published the *Art of Preserving Health*, in which he said:

> Music exacts each joy, allays each grief,
> Expels diseases, softens every pain,
> Subdues the rage of poisons and plague.

MUSICAL PHYSICIANS

The medical profession abounds in musicians, many supremely eminent in that art. Paracelsus (1453–1551), one of the pioneers of modern psychology, was also an astrologer, herbalist and musician; a fine organist, composer and instrument maker, he said that music and the making of music had immense therapeutic value. Edward Jenner (1749–1833), the originator of vaccination, performed expertly on the violin and flute, and when Dr Oliver Goldsmith (1728–74) travelled on the Continent he took with him 'one spare shirt and his flute and a single guinea'. René Laënnec (1781–1826), inventor of the stethoscope, was a fine flautist, and two of the greatest nineteenth-century musicians, Berlioz and Borodin, started their careers as doctors.

Berlioz (1803–69) loved music passionately and by the time he was 12 had mastered several wind instruments, but was forbidden to play the piano because his father thought it might wean him from the profession he had chosen for his son. He was in fact coerced into studying medicine by the promise of the finest flute that money could buy, but his heart was set on music and after a visit to the opera, where he saw *Les Danaïdes* by Salieri, he forsook medicine for composition. For the remainder of his life, however, he believed in, and preached about, the power of music to relieve stress and comfort the weary, the troubled and the sick.

Borodin (1834–87), was physician first and musician

later. This despite his musical genius, for at the age of twelve he wrote a concerto for the flute with piano accompaniment, and a string trio for two violins and cello. He was convinced that medicine was a more worthy profession, and made it his vocation, becoming one of the most brilliant students at the Academy of Medicine in St Petersburg. After obtaining his degree and working for a year in hospital he was greatly influenced by Chopin and Schumann and married a talented pianist; then he returned to the Academy where he spent the rest of his life, eventually becoming Professor of Physiological and Organic Chemistry.

Even when he was recognized as one of the foremost composers of his time he always insisted that he was 'a Sunday musician', and fled to music when the stress of work threatened to overwhelm him. 'I only compose,' he said, 'when I am too unwell to give my lectures. When my head is splitting, my eyes running, and I have to blow my nose every minute, then I give myself up to music.' And he urged others to seek relief from the same source.

Many well-known doctors have loved music and have either composed or become accomplished performers. All have realized how great is the effect of music on spirit, mind and body. Conan Doyle tells us that Sherlock Holmes, the hero of so many of his stories, sought solace and found inspiration from the violin. Nor do doctors compose classical music exclusively. 'Yankee Doodle', which most people imagine was written by an American, was the brain child of Richard Shuckburg, a British Army surgeon, who wrote it as a parody to ridicule the undisciplined American Militia; and the words and music of 'Casey Jones' were written by Dr James Naylor, of Starling College, Columbus, Ohio, who also gave us 'There'll Be A Hot Time In The Old Town Tonight'.

Almost every teaching hospital has its amateur dramatic society and its jazz band, and many run symphony orchestras. The best known of British medical musicians must be Dr Boyd Neel, who obtained a medical degree at Cambridge and then became house surgeon at St George's Hospital before building a substantial practice in South London. He too was torn between medicine and music, but unlike Borodin he refused to combine the two and gravitated to music. Few realize that he was once a medical man and imagine that 'Dr' refers to a music degree. His Boyd Neel Orchestra is famous and he, too, is a firm believer in the effects of music on health.

ALBERT SCHWEITZER

Had he chosen, Schweitzer could have been eminent in many fields: philosophy, theology, music, medicine. As a young man he was accepted as the greatest living organist, an expert in organ construction and an authority on Bach. He threw up a professional career in music to become a medical missionary in Lambaréné, in what was then French Equatorial Africa, where he brought music and medicine to his patients in the way witch doctors have done for centuries, for he proved its value in treating illnesses, especially those of the mind.

FIRST SCIENTIFIC EXPERIMENTS WITH MUSIC

Some of the first scientific experiments with music in Britain were carried out in 1880 on men and animals, but the earliest experiments in the controlled use of music in hospitals dates from 1891, when Frederick Kill Harford, a Canon of Westminster, drew up a scheme for the founding of the Guild of St Cecilia and engaged violinists and vocalists to play to any patient at the request of his medical adviser. Music was also transmitted to some wards in the main London Hospitals by telephone, which must have been the first experiment in piped music.

Months later a doctor in Manchester asked for an extension of the experiment to lunatic asylums in the North, and though both schemes were encouraged by the medical profession they were ridiculed by *musicians*! The Guild proved beyond all doubt that some cures were accelerated by music, but opposition to the scheme was so intense that it was droppped in 1896.

THE EFFECT OF MUSIC ON THE SPIRITS

When men fail to understand anything they deride it. The materialist thinks only in terms of pounds and pence, and if a satisfactory balance sheet cannot be produced he has little faith in the product. Though he protests about efficiency he fails to realize that the end product of true efficiency is happiness and contentment. Without these all the profits in the world mean nothing, as so many of the wealthy find after they have stacked up their millions.

In the Middle Ages physicians frequently called in minstrels to sing and play to patients who were ill, depressed or beset by fears and anxieties, and it was noticed that even serious afflictions often responded. Musicians and jesters were valued servants at court for laughter raises the spirits as well, and aids the healing processes.

RUDOLF STEINER

Rudolf Steiner (1861–1925), who in many ways was in advance of his time, was the founder of anthroposophy, a philosophy which attaches great importance to the spiritual way of life. He built a theatre for the performance of mystery plays and good music. 'Musical activity,' he said, 'is linked with all the vivifying forces in the human organism; it becomes associated with currents which, as it were, stream through and vivify the entire individual who thus becomes one with and, so to say, grows into union with streaming masses of sound.'

Depression is commonly supposed to be the only state dissipated by music, but it is only one of many conditions that can be alleviated or cured in this way. Nervous tension, stress, insomnia, hysteria, weak heart, a tendency to cancer, tuberculosis, epilepsy, maladjustment (usually in children) and mental illness can be relieved and, in some instances, cured.

THE HUMAN BODY IS AN INSTRUMENT

Few people realize that the human body is a musical instrument with a definite response to vibrations, though all bodies do not respond in the same way to the same music. But when the type of music is played that the body enjoys, the physical effect can be like that of massage: gentle massage when soothing rhythms are played; vigorous massage when melodies are lively. Good music makes one healthier, but bad music, even though you may like it at the time, has a harmful effect.

There must be millions – not only the young – who enjoy 'beat', 'pop' and noisy music but shy away from the classical composers, light operas and 'Old Tyme Music', for there is no accounting for the way in which minds and bodies respond to sound vibrations. Even an opera as popular as *Madame Butterfly*, which has conquered the world and is now sneered at by highbrows as being syrupy, was hooted by the audience at La Scala in Milan on its first night.

E.C. DENT: PIONEER OF MUSIC THERAPY

Dr E. C. Dent, of the Manhattan State Hospital, created a stir in medical circles in the nineteenth century when he introduced music into his wards because he found it to be of immense curative value. 'Music,' he wrote, 'consists of sound waves, and by its vibratory movements it stimulates the nerve centres, and through this channel, mainly the nervous system, the effects reach the muscular and other tissues and act as mental stimulants and restoratives. Distinct bodily action follows as the result of vibratory action of music on the auditory nerve.'

To prove his theory Dent reduced a patient's fingers to a state of complete exhaustion by voluntary movements and completed the effect by electricity so that the man could not of his own free will move his fingers. The exhaustion was local, and when slow, sad melodies were played the feeling of fatigue increased; when lively melodies were substituted, however, fatigue was reduced and eventually dispelled and his fingers returned to normal.

Dent carried out scores of experiments, some with extraordinary results. He was probably the first physician to use music for the control and cure of the mentally deranged. A woman who suffered from chronic mania and was violent and profane was placed in a straitjacket and a Chopin nocturne was played. Soon her profanity ceased and she began speaking sensibly. Under the influence of a Beethoven adagio her pulse became full and strong; and with 'Home, Sweet Home', her skin grew warm and showed a healthy reaction. Soon her nervousness disappeared and she returned to her room voluntarily and without any force being necessary. That night she slept deeply, proving the healing effect on brain and nerves. She improved rapidly under the influence of music and the straitjacket into which she had been forced was never used again.

Dent, who treated hundreds of mentally disturbed patients, said that 38 per cent recovered completely under music therapy, 33 per cent showed marked improvement, and 29 per cent showed slight improvement or were unaffected. Observation showed that music affected the rate of heartbeat, improved the action of the lungs, raised the temperature of the body slightly and had a prolonged action on the brain. Dent was so far ahead of his time that he was regarded by orthodox practitioners as a crank.

EUROPEAN THERAPISTS

Soon after, Gustav Kotte in Germany used music on patients suffering from nervous diseases to reduce the frequency of using drugs and found that music excited, exulted or soothed the listener, depending on the type played, and from this he deduced that it causes a physical reaction such as is often sought after when medicine is administered.

His contemporaries in France, Ginnet and Courtier, working on the same lines, found that lively major chords without relation to melody quickened breathing, respiration increasing according to tempo. Single notes increased the action of the heart and rapid melodies increased it further. From these experiments they concluded that music has a beneficial effect on the two most important organs, heart and lungs, and indirectly on the nervous system.

Increased action of the heart causes an increased flow of blood to all parts of the body; increased rapidity of breathing brings more oxygen into the lungs and other organs; and at the same time the lungs get rid of greater quantities of refuse such as carbonic acid gas. In short, music often acts as a tonic to invalids and may be used as a substitute when physical exercise is impossible.

Researchers often found that suitable music dissipates fatigue and brain fag. When listening to melodies the entire facial expression changes, lower limbs and hands move involuntarily to rhythm, and other muscles are affected to a lesser degree. When slow, soothing melodies were played the rate of heart beats was reduced and less blood was pumped to the brain and, as a result, sleep was induced. They proved scientifically what mothers have known instinctively for centuries when they crooned their babies to sleep with lullabies.

MUSIC A TONIC FOR FATIGUE

The businessman who returns home whacked, with a briefcase full of papers to go through, should not have a stiff whisky to pep him up, followed by a heavy meal. Instead, he should peel off his jacket, change into slippers, put on his favourite records, sit back in a comfortable chair with a cup of tea, and relax. In half an hour the meal that would have given him indigestion if eaten in a tense condition will nourish him.

Strain will disappear and he will be able to get down to work after dinner with renewed vigour and a clear mind.

MUSIC THERAPY IN AMERICA

In America, where new ideas are welcome, far more research has been conducted into music therapy than in Europe, which is conservative in outlook. During the war the Philadelphia Hospital allowed, and indeed encouraged, experiments to treat seriously ill patients with music. One of the first cases was an officer who had lain in a coma for a fortnight. After all efforts to induce consciousness had failed his bed was screened off. Then two Grey Ladies (Red Cross) offered to sing and play to him. A spinet was wheeled in and for several hours old melodies were played. Then one of them sang 'When Irish Eyes Are Smiling'. She had sung only one line when a male voice joined in – the voice of the wounded man. Music vibrations had got through to his brain when nothing else could.

Perhaps the Americans were not the first after all. Florence Nightingale obtained permission for army muscians to play the violin and other instruments to the wounded in Scutari, with excellent results, but as she was much disliked by the Brass Hats and her crackpot ideas were not pursued after the war.

THE BOOS SCHOOL

For forty years the Boos School run by E. A. and Alma Boos in Cicero, Illinois, has treated mentally ill and retarded children successfully with music. It all started when E. A. Boos, a graduate of Northwestern University, met his future wife and they decided to start their own school of music. Their first patient was a distant cousin who became mentally ill and would sit for hours in utter dejection, indifferent to surroundings and friends.

'I bought a violin,' said Boos, 'and after several failures managed to interest her in music, which she had once loved. Her restored spirits and mental improvement showed me dramatically that music has the power to unlock many doors in the human mind, whether sane or deranged.'

Their first music school was for mentally deranged children, a work they have continued ever since. Periodically a physician and a psychiatrist examine the children. Not all of them are completely cured but there have been no outright failures. One pupil was so emaciated and listless when they took him in that he had to be spoon-fed, and the attendant at the asylum from which they rescued him said: 'Why bother to feed him? In his mental state he'd be better off dead.' With their patient help, however, the boy recovered sufficiently to earn a livelihood as a farm labourer.

Among their successes are a gas-station owner, now married with several children; a shoe inspector; and a talented musician; and in between are many who now hold down jobs doing routine work.

EXPERIMENTS IN A CHICAGO HOSPITAL

About forty years ago Moissaye Boguslawski, the celebrated pianist, conducted a series of experiments in a Chicago hospital for the insane. One of his first 'patients' was an Italian mother who behaved like an animal and refused even to look at her own baby. To start with he played a number of Italian melodies from nursery rhymes to folk songs, but evoked no response. Then he began an aria from *Il Trovatore*, and before he had finished she was weeping and begging for her child.

Epilepsy is one of the diseases in which musicians have enjoyed considerable success. They find they can stop spasms from coming on if they play certain melodies before these develop. Dr L. S. Bender of the Bellevue Hospital, New York, reported several cases of mentally deranged children whose fits of violence were rapidly controlled or even terminated by soothing music. As a result of these and other experiments in American hospitals the National Association of Music Therapy was formed and musicians have sometimes cured patients when all other means have failed.

It is impossible to say which organ or organs are affected by music. The Russian Scientist Professor S. V. Kravkov, who plays many instruments, discovered that music and other sounds can sometimes improve a listener's eyesight by as much as 25 per cent. He also proved that the rhythmic ticking of a clock will stimulate the eyes. Experiments with astronomers, microscopists and engravers have resulted in their having improved vision.

ALEXANDER CANNON

Dr Alexander Cannon was labelled as a crank for most of his career because his ideas did not fit into the accepted pattern. He travelled widely in India and Tibet, practised yoga and was a keen student of the occult. When he wrote *The Invisible Influence*, in which he recorded an experience in levitation, the LCC, under whose jurisdiction he came, tried to dismiss him on grounds of mental instability, for he had branched into uncharted territory. Fortunately with the help of eminent colleagues he was able to resist them and retain his post.

During his tenure at Colney Hatch he said: 'Nice soothing music will in itself calm the troubled mind, and I have seen its marvellous effects on the insane. *Music can often do what medicine cannot.*'

We are apt to dub as mad anyone who is eccentric or acts strangely and in ways we do not understand. There may be perfectly rational explanations for those who see objects we cannot see or hear sounds to which we are oblivious. 'Some years ago,' said Cannon, 'when I bought one of the first wireless sets and allowed a certified person of unsound mind to listen to it, I was intrigued with his remark: "But do you mean, sir, that you cannot hear music without a toy instrument like that? I have heard this music at will for the past fifteen years." "*

Music abounds all around us. It is everywhere. A note once struck continues to vibrate, but normal people must have a box with a receiver inside to pick up vibrations and translate them into sound. Some people have inbuilt receivers, but because we cannot hear what they can, we call them crazy.

THE BRAIN AND SOUND

Reception of images and music depends on the condition of the brain, for all vibrations are received by the brain, from which they are dispatched to the eyes, ears and other sense-organs which convert them into images, sounds and sense-vibrations. Changes in physical conditions can make people see and hear things that are hidden from others.

In a report to the Royal Society in Berlin, a well-known bookseller named Nicolai said that for two months, while in full possession of his senses, he saw strange people passing to and fro as if they had no connection with each other; he also saw dogs, birds, and once or twice men on horseback, though none of these existed. No one else could see them. The apparitions called each other by their names and sometimes knocked on his bedroom door and asked whether other spirits lived there. His doctors were baffled. Eventually leeches were applied to his neck, a couple of pints of blood were drained off, and the apparitions ceased to appear. They must have been caused by high blood pressure which had some effect on the brain, a proof that body and mind are closely connected.

Jack Ducamp, the Human Radio Set
Medical history records cases of freaks who could hear music in the air which normal people could not. One morning, for no

* Dr Alexander Cannon, *The Invisible Influence* (Aquarian, 1969).

apparent reason, Jack Ducamp of Dalhart, Texas, suddenly began to hear music which failed to record itself on the ear-drums of his friends. His wife and friends were sceptical when he told them and began to suspect he was going mad. Eventually the family physician sent him to Dr Penny, a specialist, who examined him and took copious notes, and persuaded Ducamp to hum some of the tunes he had heard the previous day. On his next visit Penny told him: 'By some means I cannot explain, you've been listening to the short-wave (30-metre) radio station in Monterrey.' Tests made over a period of a fortnight confirmed that he was hearing music relayed from the Monterrey station at exactly the times they were broadcast.

Constant music he did not wish to hear so affected his health that he died at the age of thirty-six, and an examination of his brain revealed that it contained a growth with a number of fine membranes which responded to electrical impulses sent out on a wavelength of 30 metres! Perhaps some whom we call lunatics have similar growths inside their skulls.

In 1937 the case of Franz Skyora and Jan Vltavasky, foundry workers in Marisch-Ostrau, Czechoslovakia, was a seven-day wonder. Quite by accident they found that when they clasped hands their bodies were converted into a radio receiving station, and that others could hear the music, too. The local radio club was informed and scientists at Prague University agreed to test them. The scientists confirmed that when the men held hands they received music from a number of radio stations, but could advance no logical explanation.

Within the last forty years a great deal has been discovered about the effects of music on the sick and the insane. William van de Wall, a Dutch psychiatrist and expert in music therapy, practising in America, obtained permission to enter a room in which a violent, powerfully-built inmate was kept, – a man noted for his vicious attacks on warders. He entered alone, carrying a portable organ which he played while he sang. The man was about to hurl himself at van de Wall, but the music seemed to calm him and he soon joined in the singing. For a week van de Wall sang and played to the patient, who after a few months was moved from the violent ward. Eventually his sanity was restored and he became a useful member of society.

Dr C. de Radwan, a Polish psychologist who founded the Institute of Psychophony in London in the Thirties, also had remarkable success in treating neurasthenics and the mentally unbalanced by what he called 'psychic vibrations' and sound. He was scoffed at when he started but built up a large practice and was a pioneer of music therapy in Britain.

SOCIETY FOR MUSIC THERAPY

In 1958 the Society for Music Therapy and Remedial Music was formed by Miss Juliette Alvin, a cellist who has had considerable experience in this kind of work and has written a book on her experiences.* She was helped by Norah Gruhn, widow of Dr Sidney Mitchell, of Warlingham Park Hospital, and later of Cane Hill Mental Hospital, Surrey.

MUSIC IN BRITISH HOSPITALS

Mr John Wilder, General Secretary of the Psychiatric and Rehabilitation Association, said in 1964 that music provides a relief from stress and self-pity and results in greater friendliness between patients and staff. The Rev. T. H. Lovegrove, Warden of Sherrards Training Centre for Spastics, stated that it provides a stimulus to creative activity.

In 1962 a report in *Hospital and Health Management* stated that patients like to hear softly played background music, and music is now relayed in waiting rooms, wards, labour rooms and physiotherapy departments in six London hospitals. The most popular are light classical music, waltzes and orchestral pieces; the most disliked by the sick are marches, Latin-American music and foxtrots. Patients say

* Juliette Alvin, *Music For The Handicapped Child* (Oxford University Press, 1965).

that music takes their minds off hospital smells, relieves boredom and makes hospitals more human. Soft music has the effect of lulling patients off to sleep. Patients have earphones which they can switch on and off, and in many hospitals they can tune in to programmes of their choice, for nothing irritates more than having to listen to music one dislikes.

A group from Erlanger University, Munich, while investigating ulcers and stomach upsets, found that sixty patients in a test group reacted favourably to Beethoven and Mozart, and a few even to rock music, which seemed to 'lull' their acid stomachs after thirty to sixty minutes.

The periodical *MD*, February 1958, stated that obstetricians and gynaecologists have found that if soft music is played in a minor key to pregnant mothers the need for premedication can be reduced when they are about to give birth. Powerful anaesthetics sometimes cause irreparable damage to both mother and child, and any reduction in drugs is welcome.

OPERATIONS UNDER MUSIC

The right kind of music can anaesthetize, though few fall completely under its spell. In 1956 a South African doctor in London experimented with a gas-plus-music technique and found that the state of unconsciousness was longer and deeper, the process of 'going under' more pleasant, weaker anaesthetics could be administered, and the after-effects were negligible. He even found that patients could be given a meal before the operation without subsequent harm. This led others to believe that patients could be put to sleep by music alone, without the aid of anaesthetics, and a paper on the subject was published.*

In 1961 a group of doctors at the Odstock Hospital, Salisbury, performed hundreds of operations where patients were put under by a combination of music and local anaesthetics. And in 1962 the first major operation was carried out with

* *Journal of the Association of Anaesthetists*, April 1956.

music as the sole anaesthetic, when Pierre Savineau, a yacht captain, had his appendix removed to the strains of Tchaikovsky concertos, and the operation was televised throughout France. During the seventeen minutes it occupied he chatted to the surgeon and when it was completed he left the theatre on the arm of a nurse. But the use of music as an anaesthetic will never become universal because millions will not be deeply enough affected to fall asleep under its influence, and if they did, might wake with alarm at the first slice of the scalpel.

Sound has long been recognized as the most occult of the sense stimulants and the suggestive effect of many rhythms is hypnotic, for the vibrations of soothing music and the sibilant formulae used by hypnotists have much in common.

Medical men and musicians now recognize the value of music as an aid during illness and are collaborating with enthusiasm, but not all methods are equally successful with all patients. Dr Walter Kluge, the eminent German psychoanalyst, experimented with melodies till he found one that particularly pleased his patient, and this was repeated again and again till he abandoned all resistance. When that happened he could delve into the patient's mind freely and extract from him the fears and anxieties which lay in his subconscious.

SING IN YOUR BATH

Music, whether vocal or instrumental, is good for all. The joy and uplift engendered causes the glands to secrete health-giving hormones into the bloodstream and affords emotional release. It restores balance and produces a harmonious outlook.

Singing is always beneficial, even though you may not have a melodious voice or cannot sing in tune. It expands the lungs and improves breathing. Your singing may bring groans and shudders from your family and friends but it is good for you, whether you sing alone, in a group, or in your bath.

When you sing in your bath your voice always sounds better

than it really is – in fact, a feeble voice may sound magnificent to the performer and enable him to express himself, increasing his ego. The hard surfaces in the bathroom reinforce the weakest voices and give them a timbre and resonance otherwise lacking. Of late this branch of singing has attracted the attention of psychologists, who say that singing in the bathtub should never be repressed. It is good for body, mind and spirit.

Never scorn music of any kind, or those who revel in the sort of music that pains you, for they get pleasure and gain benefit from it. A few like dining in silence, or read as they eat, but the digestions of most people respond when they eat to the accompaniment of music. The great feasts of the Greeks and Romans would have been incomplete without music, and Epictetus said that a table without music is a manger. The kind of music you like, played softly, can aid digestion.

6
How Music Influences
Human Behaviour

Within the last fifty years it has dawned on us that music is not only for pleasure, or to lift our spirits when depressed, or help us to get better when we fall ill. It has wider uses, industrially and politically.

That music influences the behaviour of men and animals, and sometimes plants, there is little doubt. Professor T. C. N. Singh, Professor of Botany at Annamalai University, South India, has found that if soft music is broadcast for a few hours each day certain crops grow faster and get bigger. He also found that the ringing of an electric bell can so excite seeds that they sprout faster. His theories were tested for two years by agricultural experts, who said that crops of paddy (rice) increased by nearly 30 per cent and the straw yield went up by 75 per cent.

When Dr Singh played violin serenades to a 6-acre tobacco plantation for two months, plants nearest the music grew much faster than those further away. When he played to rice crops, plants within the range of music grew 15 inches higher than those outside it.

According to *Medical Press*, an Indian publication, some plants grow faster and taller if music is played to them every day, and experiments are being carried out using various kinds of music on a variety of plants at the Delhi Agricultural Institute and at the sound laboratory, Benaras, where research into music therapy is headed by the well-known vocalist Pandit Omkarnath Thakore and the Italian musician, Alain Danjelou.

More than fifty years ago Luther Burbank, the American horticulturist, said that when he spoke in kindly tones to his plants they responded by producing bigger and better blooms; so they called him a crank.

MUSIC AND INDUSTRY

The idea that music can increase efficiency in factories and offices was thought of centuries before the BBC launched their programme 'Music While You Work'. It is common knowledge that slaves who built the pyramids sang work chants as they hauled the gigantic blocks of stone into position. We know that the Greeks had special work songs for harvesting, threshing, grinding corn, spinning and weaving. Music has always been part of the life of Negroes all over Africa. In Liberia every village has its orchestra and choir and people constantly improvise new songs and invent new instruments. When the slaves were taken to the Americas they invented their own folk music and grafted it on to American culture. They made up songs which they sang in unison to relieve drudgery and raise their spirits.

Russian serfs sang as they pulled barges up river and the 'Song of The Volga Boatman' is based on work music. In the days of sail, sea shanties served the same purpose. Many have been preserved and are sung in music halls, pubs and elsewhere for pleasure. Without such music hard labour and repetitive work would be unbearable.

CHANTING IN THE EAST

Chants have been used throughout the East since the dawn of

time. As a boy it thrilled me to listen to the melodious chanting of the river pilots on the Ganges as they heaved the lead and sang out the depth, and to gangs of coolies singing in chorus as they raised or hauled heavy objects. The leading man would sing out a line or two to urge them on and the remainder would join in a rousing chorus.

Later I listened with fascination to the rhythmic chants as men worked in pairs screwing water tubes into boilers in a power station in Kanchrapara, Eastern Bengal, and carried out other tasks involving team work. Their chants had rhythm, melody and changes in tempo and helped to synchronize mind and body, coordinate the muscles, elevate the spirits, regulate breath and ward off fatigue. Working chants often originate spontaneously because singing is natural and more often than not words are improvised to suit the occasion. Often they are bawdy and give rise to laughter, which always raises the spirits.

MUSIC IN INDUSTRY

The earliest experiments with music as an aid to business efficiency were conducted in the Latin-American countries, where it is regarded almost as a form of nourishment. Cuban cigar workers, for instance, invariably worked to music of some kind – usually guitar or mandoline – and after the advent of radio, to symphonies and operas.

Today machines do most of the heavy work that men did in the past. Machines have brought about mass production, than which there is nothing more boring and fatiguing. Since the invention of radio, music has been brought within the reach of all and it has been introduced into shops, offices and factories to banish boredom, reduce fatigue, increase output and keep workers happy. If played softly it does not intrude on the senses and workers can hum or sing in time with it. As a general rule women, who do most of the repetitive jobs, appreciate music more than men. It has been proved that music keeps workers happy and improves their efficiency even though they may not listen consciously. It impinges on the eardrums and acts involuntarily through the nervous system, provided it is not played loudly.

NATIONAL INSTITUTE OF INDUSTRIAL PSYCHOLOGY

In the early days of experiments with music in industry, researchers from the National Institute of Industrial Psychology interviewed officials in 1050 factories employing a total of 300,000 people. Managers observed that men working with hammers kept time to 'swingy' music. Where girls were employed it had the effect of stopping chatter and increased output. Many girls preferred to work in warehouses where music was provided than in offices where it was not, even though the pay in offices was higher, which proved that often a pleasing environment is preferable to more money. Where singing was permitted they could not gossip and got through more work. Where both slow and fast music was played, output varied as girls tended to work to the speed of the beat.

The report stated: 'We must not condemn canned music too harshly, for its presence in the factory may be the modern equivalent to the flute player of olden days who charmed the ears of the Greek ladies as they carried out their household tasks.'

VAN DEN BERG'S EXPERIMENT

J. P. Van Den Berg, managing director of the great margarine firm, said that from the start music in their factories was an unqualified success, but that the types of music favoured by girls and men differed. Girls liked straight dance tunes, sentimental numbers, old-fashioned waltzes and comedy chorus numbers in that order; men preferred straight dance tunes, hot swing numbers, comedy chorus numbers, sentimental numbers and old-fashioned music. The most popular time for music was just after breakfast, when snappy dance tunes were favourites with the girls and military bands with the men.

A fruit factory in Kent found that production increased by 30 per cent when music was introduced, and even bricklayers pepped up their output when music was relayed to them. It was found that if music is piped to a factory and then discontinued the workers – especially girls – miss it. In 1951 fifty girls in a Belfast factory went on strike because music was stopped, and the management was forced to reintroduce it.

THE COOPERATIVE EXPERIMENT

In 1971 the Cooperative Wholesale Society in Manchester was worried about its 'date origination department', the mainspring of its computer system, because 120 girls who produced 11 miles of punched tape a day working at 'a high performance level' were making 8.1 per cent of errors and the sickness rate rose to 7.25 per cent.

On advice the management introduced piped music to counteract the noise of machines and reduce errors and absenteeism. Within four weeks the percentage of errors fell to 5.7, the sickness rate to 5.6. Music had been relayed unobtrusively for periods of fifteen minutes with fifteen-minute intervals of silence.

D. P. SMITH'S EXPERIMENT

Music in places of work was introduced into America by D. P. Smith of the Insurance Co., Oakland, California, a man of vision and judgement and a lover of good music, who was convinced that it would reduce strain. He was the first man to instal RCA System Sound Projectors and pipe music throughout the building. His original collection, which was carefully thought out, consisted of two hundred selections of waltzes, college songs, jingles, marches, orchestral pieces, vocal solos and religious and symphonic music. Marches and snappy tunes were played during the first hour of the day, during the lunch period and when workers clocked off, as it was during these periods that there was a mental lag in physical and mental energy. At all other times subdued and quiet music was relayed.

Observers were surprised to see that gloomy faces were transformed to happy ones when tunes such as 'Jingle Bells', 'Whistle While You Work', and 'Anchors Aweigh', were played. After the novelty wore off he began to get requests for favourite selections, and as a result business efficiency increased because the staff was happier.

Then the Iatz Advertising Service of New York decided to instal piped music in their offices to cope with an overwhelming rush of orders, and production rose by 20 per cent. When the rush was over they found that music maintained production by just over 10 per cent of normal.

MUSIC COUNTERACTS FATIGUE

Hundreds of offices and factories then decided to relay music, and it was even installed at Madison Square Garden during a six-day cycle race. Music was played for forty-six minutes, followed by an interval of silence for forty-six minutes. It was found that the average speed during music periods was 19.6 mph, and during periods of silence 17.9 mph, proving conclusively that the right sort of music dissipates fatigue and the monotony which causes it, and enables muscles to co-ordinate more efficiently.

This is true not only of commerce and industry but of work of every description. The famous German surgeon Bilroth always operated far more brilliantly after attending a symphony concert, and before the days when masks were worn, many surgeons sang as they operated.

THE EMOTIONAL IMPACT OF MUSIC

Not everyone is moved to the same degree by music, and one would not go all the way with Shakespeare when he said:

> The man that hath no music in himself,
> Nor is not mov'd with concord of sweet sounds,
> Is fit for treasons, stratagems and spoils . . .

for there are many admirable people on whom music makes no impact whatever, and in those who are influenced it produces a variety of emotions. Some are moved to laughter and some to tears, which the Anglo-Saxon is so loth to be seen shedding, but which are a valuable therapeutic outlet. Because the British do not weep easily and keep 'a stiff upper lip' their emotions remain bottled. As a result they suffer more from stress than volatile races, such as Greeks and Italians, who laugh, weep and fly into rages at what we would term trivialities, and so rid themselves of repressions and inhibitions.

One of the blessings of the cinema is that, under a cloak of darkness, romantic music and a flood of sentimentality makes most women weep copiously and it is not uncommon to hear them say on their return home: 'It was wonderful. I wept buckets!'

Pent-up emotions are released along with tears, and music is the prime instrument of their release. One should not be ashamed of weeping when really moved.

MARTIAL MUSIC

The purpose of martial music is to put new life into men so weary that they can hardly drag one foot after the other, to make them march 20 miles when 10 seem the limit of endurance, to send them into action with pulses racing, and to instil them with patriotic fervour. No one who is not tone-deaf can help tapping his feet or keeping time with his hands to a Souza march, or prevent blood coursing faster through his veins. Music promotes reflex action over which one has no control. Experience has shown that men will march with a livelier step behind a band than without one. Those who organize armies know this and spend large sums on bands and the training of musicians. Even the bagpipes have a purpose, if only to demoralize the enemy.

GENERAL TOM BRIDGES AND HIS DRUM

When during the Battle of Mons in 1918 General Tom Bridges entered a town square he was aghast to see groups of men lying about so exhausted that they ignored his commands. Threats of court martial and punishment made no difference, for they had been fighting for days and were at the end of their physical resources.

The Germans were on the outskirts of the town and advancing, and he realized that if the men did not move they would be killed or taken prisoner. Drastic measures were needed to jerk them into activity. As commands and cajolery had failed he went into a corner shop and returned with a child's drum, on which he beat a brisk tattoo. This seemed to inject new life into the men, who rose in twos and threes, clutched their rifles, fell into line and marched behind him into the temporary shelter of reserved trenches.

HOW THE NAZIS BEMUSED OSLO

In the past, music has been used not only to soothe and heal but to enrage and whip up emotions for military and political purposes. Among those who have paid tribute to its hidden powers is Pope, who wrote:

> Light quirks of music, broken and uneven,
> Make the soul dance a jig to heaven.

The Nazis may not have read Pope, but they too knew the awful fascination of music, for on 16 April 1940 they insinuated into Oslo a twelve-piece military band and two men with accordions, who played rousing soldiers' choruses, typical rollicking music that went with a swing and made the people gather round, clap their hands, stamp their feet and join in. Concerts were staged alongside the Carl Johan Boulevard in the centre of the city and thousands of Norwegians joined enthusiastically in a jovial rendition of 'Roll Out The Barrel' and other traditional drinking songs. While the citizens were hypnotized by music and song, small bands of armed Nazis numbering 20,000 altogether disembarked unobtrusively from boats over a period of about three days and, mingling with the people, took up key positions throughout the city.

Some of the Nazis even led the singing, shouting the words of 'Going To Town', a Teuton melody which gains maximum syncopation from the accordion. The Germans acted like carefree students who were there to have fun and give the people a good time, whereas in reality they were taking them into thrall. By the time the natives had recovered their wits Oslo had been taken over by one of the best-thought-out psychological ploys in history. Today those two songs are among the most hated in Norway and are never played or sung in public.

The approach to Oslo was guarded by powerful guns on the heights overlooking the harbour. Had the Nazis attacked in convoys of troops escorted by battleships they would probably have captured Oslo anyway, but only at the cost of thousands of lives and the opening of a second front. As it was, music and song gained them a bloodless victory.

WARS MUST HAVE THEIR MUSIC

Every war throws up its popular tunes which help men to fight and endure and give them a little pleasure in the midst of hardship and misery. In 1914 'It's A Long Way To Tipperary' caught the fancy of British troops in Flanders; in 1942 'Lili Marlene', composed by a German, was the song of the British in North Africa.

During the French Revolution in 1792 Claude Rouget de Lisle, a French royalist, was dismayed at the apathy of the Republican troops facing the Prussians, so on 24 April, after dining and with a bottle of old Rhine wine to inspire him, he wrote '*Chant de l'Armée du Rhin*', intending it to be a patriotic song. The following August it was sung during an attack on the Tuileries, spread through the army and became the national anthem of France. It is perhaps the most stirring of all national anthems.

THE ANTHEM OF HATE

The 'Horst Wessel Song' which during Nazi concerts always followed '*Deutschland Über Alles*' was written in October 1917 by a law student, a hater of Jews and Communists, who were making their presence felt. When the Nazis swept into power he became their idol and would probably have become one of their leaders had he not been struck down on 14 January 1930 by a stray bullet. As he lay dying he was offered the services of a Jewish doctor but spurned aid from such a hated source. This made him a martyr and a hero, and his song became the anthem of the Nazis.

It was first sung as an anthem when 107 Nazi deputies stormed into the Reichstag in protest against Dr Bruning's policy, and was taken over by the *Bund Deutscher Mädels*. Girls and boys yelled it with lunatic passion and arms outstretched in the Hitler salute.

SONG THAT BROUGHT THE DEATH PENALTY

Edouard Remenyi (1830–98), who was sentenced to death

no fewer than six times for playing to his people, was one of the greatest of Hungarian violinists. Beethoven said: 'Music should strike fire from the heart of Man, and bring tears to the eyes of Woman.' This the music of Remenyi did – and it made him a national hero. During the Austro-Hungarian War of 1848 his music so inflamed his countrymen, causing them to rebel, that he was compelled to go into hiding and was sentenced to death *in absentia* by various courts, but his people hid and sheltered him and he defied the authorities and continued playing.

WHEN EUROPE WAS SAVED BY A SONG

Those who consider modern wars the most devastating in history would shudder if they read the story of the Thirty Years War which raged in Europe during the seventeenth century, for the excesses of the men in power vie with those of the Nazis. Twenty-five per cent of the population was wiped out and men thought that the end of the world had come.

At St Ulrich, a suburb of Vienna, a huge pit was filled with plague victims and into this was hurled the 'dead' body of an itinerant street singer named Augustin. Fortunately he was merely 'dead drunk' and sobered up at dawn, when he emerged, drew a bottle from his pocket, took a long swig and burst into a merry song called '*Ach! Du Lieber Augustin!*' As if by a miracle a crowd gathered, men and women started to sing, cheer and dance and the pall of doom which overhung the city seemed to lift. The tune, a catchy one, spread, and wherever it was sung men breathed new hope and turned to their labours with renewed vigour, proving Henry Clay Work right when he wrote:

Bring the good old bugle, boys! we'll sing another
    song –
Sing it with a spirit that will start the world
    along . . .

THE MORBID POWER OF SONG

Song can elevate the spirits but it can also depress them. In 1937 Rezso Javor quarrelled with his sweetheart, who committed suicide. He sat by her grave and in a fit of despair wrote 'Sadly one Sunday I waited and waited . . .' Laszlo Seress composed the music for the lyric, records made of it sold by the hundred thousand and between them they netted £40,000, which in post-war Hungary was a tidy fortune.

No one could account for the popularity of this dirge, which within a few weeks was responsible for twenty suicides, for beside the bed of each victim was found a gramophone with this record on the turntable. It had such a fascination for the depressed that the police prevailed on the authorities to ban it.

It was introduced into Britain, where the BBC broadcast it as a 'straight' ballad, but as again it left a trail of suicides disc jockeys were forbidden to play it. Most of the suicides were teenage girls who took their romances with deadly seriousness, an exception being an elderly shoemaker who left a note asking for a hundred roses, mentioned in the song, to be placed on his grave. 'Gloomy Sunday' crossed the Atlantic to the USA, where the toll of suicides was even greater and it was eventually banned.

Songs can have all sorts of repercussions. Servicemen know, for instance, that the innocent whistling of 'Colonel Bogey' as the sergeant-major makes his rounds can make that officer's hair bristle with rage so great that all within range are in danger of being placed on a charge. Yet, the song is a stirring one and is often played on official occasions.

THE FIREMEN OF VIGGUI

Shortly after the 1914 war the composer Armando Fragna wrote the words and music of 'The Firemen of Viggui', which was not intended to be taken seriously. It described how the firemen of that town wore comic-opera uniforms with red and blue feathered caps and were downcast because there were no

fires to enable them to show off their splendour, so they set fire
to the town hall and tried to dowse it with petrol. The tune
was catchy and the lyric lilting. The radio blared it incessantly
and soon all Italy was humming and singing it. This infuri-
ated the firemen of Viggui, who felt that the song was an
insult to their profession, so they and all the other firemen in
the country threatened to go on strike unless it was banned —
and banned it was.

THE POWER OF MUSIC TO
AROUSE PASSIONS

The power that music has of transforming men into frenzied
animals was realized by primitive tribes early in the history of
mankind. It is still a force to be reckoned with in Africa, where
tribal dances last for hours, sometimes days, and docile men
are turned into demons seething with rage and the desire to
kill and plunder.

This has happened in Europe also. In 1937 after a chorus
festival in the Croat town of Senj, the Nationalists demonstrated against the King and the State by singing revolutionary Croat songs which so worked up the people that they
went berserk, killing six royalists, severely wounding six
others and leaving behind a trail of two hundred with minor
injuries. The military were called out to suppress the rising,
more lives were lost and all revolutionary songs were banned.

'AMAR SONAR BANGLA'

The most recent example of a revolutionary song being
banned was '*Amar Sonar Bangla*' (My Golden Bengal), written by Rabindranath Tagore, poet and philosopher, who won
a Nobel Prize for literature. He also wrote India's national
anthem. When Sheikh Mujib Rahman, who became the first

Prime Minister of Bangladesh, was slapped into jail by the oppressive Pakistan regime, '*Amar Sonar Bangla*' was sung with patriotic fervour by all who hated the government, so it was promptly banned, along with all Tagore's songs and poems. But when the new nation arose after the oppressors were overthrown, it became the national anthem.

MUSIC CAN ALSO ENERVATE

There can be little doubt that the traditional music of Hawaii has contributed towards making the people of the islands peaceful and pleasure loving. The same may be true of Italy, for who wants to fight when he can listen to and sing the haunting melodies played there? Domenico Cimarosa (1749–1801), who between 1774 and 1787 wrote forty-seven successful grand operas and innumerable songs, for which he was honoured by Catherine II of Russia and the Emperor Josef of Austria, was exiled from his country by King Ferdinand because his music was so soothing and haunting that it sapped men's desire for war and caused the army to lose its offensive spirit. Would that such music were universal today! The Italians are great lovers of music and when they go to war they take their instruments with them as part of their equipment. Because they did so British troops in North Africa were regaled by some of the most enchanting music, played by prisoners of war, that they had ever heard.

Music also scared the authorities in South Vietnam who discovered that certain songs were undermining the will of the people to fight. In 1963 the Director of Information stated that 'music and lyrics have the value of bullets', and banned eighty-five songs that were turning people from their struggle and their thoughts to peace. The combination of music and a bad cause helped in their defeat. Among the songs banned were 'Aimless Loitering At Dusk', 'Flowers Swept Away by Rushing Waters' and 'Where To Find Compassion'.

The English are a phlegmatic people, and one has to cross the border into Wales for a rugger match to realize how crowds can be stirred by the massed singing of 'Cwm Rhondda' and 'Sospan Fach', which have inspired many a Welsh side to victory.

MUSIC AS A POLITICAL WEAPON

In America, which has a strong Teutonic and Latin amalgam of races, music is used by political parties to batter down the resistance of the opposition. At open-air meetings pretty majorettes in exotic uniforms accompanied by brass bands stir up emotion. Conventions usually start with an aria by a contralto from the Metropolitan Opera House to put the audience in the right frame of mind, followed by invocations from a minister, a priest and a rabbi in turn. At one convention Will Rogers, the homespun philosopher, tried to persuade Madame Schumann-Heink the famous opera singer to *sing* the keynote speech!

In 1956, for instance, the introduction of the candidate was followed by the Manny Harmon Orchestra, then State College Songs, and the Loring Club Male Chorus singing 'Real Nice Clambake', the Young Republican Pom-Pom Girls, Lucille Norman with an Irving Berlin Medley and finally by John Charles Thomas rendering 'The Battle Hymn of The Republic'. Only when the natives were worked into a state of patriotic frenzy and thoroughly softened up were the politicians let loose with their speeches.

The principle is exactly the same as that adopted by primitive tribes in Africa.

MUSIC BREAKS DOWN RESISTANCE

Masses behave very differently from individuals. The individual thinks and decides his own course but when surrounded by others their vibrations induce him to think and act as they do. The instinct is atavistic. If one animal in a herd panics, the remainder are likely to stampede.

This politicians in America seem to know and important contenders for the presidency are greeted by their favourite tunes, repeated *ad nauseam*. Mrs Wilkie, wife of Wendell Wilkie, had 'Let Me Call You Sweetheart' played to her audiences till they were dizzy; Taft's captive crowds were battered by 'I'm Looking Over A Four-Leaf Clover' 4000 times in four days; Al Smith's by 'Sidewalks Of New York'; Kefauver's by 'The Tennessee Waltz', and Truman's by 'Missouri Waltz'.

When a president is elected he is invariably greeted with 'Hail To The Chief'. No wonder a bewildered French newspaperman asked: 'How can I explain to readers what all this had to do with electing a President?'* He failed to realize that mass-music produces the right degree of charisma and hypnotizes people into voting for the man on the dais.

Roosevelt was swept into power for his second term by 'Happy Days Are Here Again', despite the fact that his opponents played 'Oh! Susanna!' 1800 times in six days in one hall alone. It is a wonder that the walls did not crumble. They lost. They deserved to.

W. LEE O'DANIELL

W. Lee O'Daniell, the millionaire flour mill owner who stood for governor in Texas in 1938, was a firm believer in the power of music to gain political office. The idea of offering himself as a candidate was put into his head by a blind man who asked him to stand. He read the letter to a radio audience and asked their opinion, and within a week received 54,499 letters begging him to stand, and only three urging him not to. His mind was made up, and he took his Hill Billy Band and

* Robert Bendiner, *White House Fever* (Methuen, 1960).

the sound truck he used for promoting sales of flour and set off on a thirty-six day campaign trip. Every newspaper in Texas opposed him.

E. J. Davis had been governor since the oldest voter could remember, and his nomination was considered the equivalent of an election victory. But they reckoned without the power of music and Irish blarney. Wherever Lee O'Daniell went he said he was going to run on the Ten Commandments and when asked how, he would smile and say: 'Well, take the fourth commandment – "Honour thy father and thy mother" – doesn't that mean old age pensions just as plain as day?'

Each day he plugged the songs 'I've Got That Million Dollar Smile', 'Pass The Biscuits, Pappy' (plugging his own products) and 'The Boy Who Never Got Too Old To Comb His Mother's Hair'. He had no policy whatever, but a combination of music, song and mawkish sentimentality did the trick. He waltzed home with 30,000 votes, more than those of all his opponents put together.

MUSIC AND RELIGION

All the great religions use music to induce a feeling of reverence and the right kind of atmosphere. The Roman Catholic Church, which for centuries has conducted services and singing in Latin, a language incomprehensible to most people, might have collapsed long ago but for the resonant, melodious chanting by priests specially trained in the art, which conveys a feeling of piety and the presence of an all-powerful deity. And no instrument is better suited to doing this than the organ.

The value of the litanies and responses which play so important a part in the Anglican service, lies in sound and repetition. Repeated frequently as they are, they cause the suppliant to breathe deeply and produce health-giving vibrations.

SIR PAUL DUKES

Sir Paul Dukes said that when he was in Russia during the First World War he was taught the full significance of the Lord's Prayer by a revolutionary. With hands folded in his lap his teacher inhaled slowly and deeply, retained his breath for a few moments and then began in 'a low, rich, musical bass note, about G2 below middle C.' The sound reverberated throughout the room. 'From start to finish there was no stop, no hesitation, no halt for breath, no rise or fall in tone; it was one single sound, integral and self-contained, imparting to the prayer a meaning far deeper than the words themselves. The word *amen* – pronounced, of course, *ah-meen* – trailed off into inaudibility in a way that merged the fading musical note with the ensuing silence. Chanted slowly in a single breath it seemed to last a very long time.'*

The words were relatively unimportant. They were a convenient measure for a single breath which produced the right vibrations for meditation and health.

Sir Paul said: 'I placed the tips of my fingers at the base of his chest. He drew a deep breath and began to intone approximately the same note as before. I felt his entire torso vibrating, and the vibration was communicated to me rather like a mild electric current.'

The effect was similar to that produced by Buddhists when they chant the mantra OM. Chanting, toning and singing also play a significant part in the Jewish religious service and ceremonies, which cannot fail to impress any who have heard them.

The ritual which accompanies singing is important and acts as a mild form of exercise. This is stressed in Muslim services, where the bending, kneeling, placing the head on the floor and rising, all repeated many times, help to keep the body fit and lissom.

The eerie cry of the muzzin: 'La ilaha illa Allah!' (There is no god but Allah) from the tower of the mosque in the early

---

*Sir Paul Dukes, *The Yoga of Health, Youth and Joy* (Cassell, 1960).

morning and at eventide, calling the faithful to prayer, once heard is never forgotten. Nor is the sound of the conches from Hindu and Buddhist temples, which split the air like the voices of doom.

Brass bands and singing also play an important part in all Salvation Army services, many of which are held in the open air and at street corners. The music attracts, usually children and loiterers. The moment they join in they become participants, and the singing followed by an exhortation softens them up. In this way many are brought into the fold. Often their missionaries enter pubs and start singing and the customers join in and, as their inhibitions have been dissipated by beer and spirits, they usually put their hands into their pockets for a good cause. Without music the Salvation Army would collapse.

7
Vibrations and Astrology

MUSIC AND ASTROLOGY

Till recently it was fashionable to decry astrology, which fell into disrepute in the eighteenth and nineteenth centuries, the ages of scientific materialism, but in the last fifty years a growing body of opinion has come round to the view that it is worth investigating, and an increasing number of homeopaths, herbalists, naturopaths, chiropractors, osteopaths and even orthodox medical men are convinced that vibrations from the planets influence all forms of life on earth and that these effects vary with the courses of the planets in their orbits round the sun.

FRANK A. BROWN

Frank A. Brown, Professor of Biology at Northwestern University, Evanston, Illinois, has carried out hundreds of experiments with root vegetables and has endorsed Steiner's findings that they absorb oxygen and grow at varying rates according to the daily positions of the Moon. And Professor Michel Gauquelin, who decided to collect details of the births of famous people and relate them to their professions with the idea of discounting astrology, ended by finding it was true!

He set out twenty years ago by studying the birth times of 500 eminent French physicians and surgeons and found that a disproportionately large number were born with Mars or Saturn just rising or at their zenith. This unexpected result so shook his beliefs that he collected the same information for 500 other doctors and came to the same conclusions. Still unconvinced, he collected the birth times of 25,000 well-known people in Germany, France, Italy, Belgium and Holland, and when their horoscopes were calculated his earlier findings were confirmed. He found, without exception, that those eminent in any profession invariably had certain planets rising or at their zenith at the time of birth. Doctors, soldiers and athletes all had Mars on the horizon or when it had just passed the mid heaven, politicians had Jupiter in these positions, scientists had Saturn, and writers had the Moon similarly placed.

Pursuing his research further he consulted the birth registers in Paris and compared the planetary positions of 15,000 children with those of their parents – in all more than 300,000 planetary positions. In every instance his previous findings were confirmed, though the odds against this being so are 'astronomical'. He was forced reluctantly to the conclusion that vibrations from the planets influence to an extraordinary degree the behaviour of every human being on earth.

ASTROLOGY AND MUSIC

No two persons are exactly the same, though in the cases of identical twins the variations are extremely slight. Differences depend on times and places of birth, and even identical twins are not born at precisely the same moment, while as far as ordinary twins are concerned there may be a considerable gap between births. Mrs Frank Castro of Levelland, Texas, gave birth to a son on 8 December 1967 and to a daughter a month later;* a mother at the Motala Municipal Maternity Home in

* *Guardian*: 11 January 1967.

Sweden gave birth to a daughter on 1 November 1968 and to a twin six weeks later;* and in Sydney there is recorded a gap of fifty-six days between twins.

According to astrology identical twins think, feel and act alike, and others born in different places and times have different ideas, feelings and inclinations. Which accounts, among others things, for their wide divergencies in music. Those who like one type of music often cannot understand why others like an entirely different type which they find it hard to tolerate. The moment you understand the reason, however, you will not condemn or regard the choice of another with contempt or wonder why he (or she) is not affected in the same way by your kind of music.

PAUL FOSTER CASE

Considerable research into music and astrological types has been carried out in America by Professor Paul Foster Case, who found that each sign corresponds to one or more keys in the tonal scale. He gives a rough idea of the kinds of music which appeal to the various types and soothes them when tense and under strain – a rough idea because he deals only with the Sun signs, or the sign at the exact moment of birth, which almost invariably has a powerful influence on the 'native', the person whose horoscope is being read.

Aries (21 March–20 April): a fiery type who like to lead and dominate and whose vibratory nature responds best to the key of C-natural, which soothes them. Since Mars rules the muscles and blood corpuscles, some music will relieve tension, headaches and stress.

Beethoven's Sonata No. 21 in C; Mozart's Symphony No. 34 in C; Schubert's Symphony No. 9 in C and similar music.

Taurus (21 April–20 May): Taureans are natural music lovers and some of the greatest singers and musicians, such as Caruso, Dame Nellie Melba, Bing Crosby, Yehudi Menuhin and Burt Bacharach, were born under this sign. It is almost

* *Guardian*: 10 December 1968.

impossible to excel in opera without Taurus being strong in
the chart, for among other things Taurus rules the throat,
neck and ears. Though Taureans dislike noise they have a tendency to play their music a trifle too loudly, but are soothed by
music in C-sharp and D-flat.

Beethoven's Sonata No. 14 in C-sharp minor, Opus 27, No.
2; Chopin's Nocturne in C-sharp; Mahler's Symphony No. 5
in C-sharp; Prokofiev's Concerto No. 1 in D-flat for piano,
Op. 10.

Gemini (21 May–21 June): Geminians are lovers of noise.
No sooner do they settle in the driving seat of a car then they
turn on the radio. When home from work they turn on radio
or TV before anything else. More often than not they pay little
attention to what is being played, but let any member of the
family turn off the sound and they want to know the reason.
They must have something going on. They are compulsive
listeners because their nervous systems are so highly developed
that they are always keyed up. They more often than others
tend to have nervous breakdowns and they respond best to
music in D-natural. All music played in this key has a good
effect on them.

Bach's Magnificat in D; Mahler's Symphony No. 9 in D;
Mozart's 'Haffner Serenade' in D.

Cancer (22 June–22 July): generally speaking these are
tolerant, home-loving sentimentalists, attached to family and
country; lovers of traditional and the established order. They
are controlled by their emotions, for Cancer governs the chest,
stomach, liver, pancreas and solar plexus, the seat of the emotions. They respond best to music in D-sharp and E-flat.

Bach's Praeludium, Fugue and Allegro in E-flat major, S.
998; Beethoven's Concerto No. 5 in E-flat, Op. 73
('Emperor'); Haydn's Sonata in E-flat.

Leo (23 July–22 August): like Aries these natives are bold
in thought and action and make good leaders. Though they do
not love noise for the sake of noise, their music must be played
loudly. Souza, for instance, probably had Leo rising or strong
in his chart. Though they like popular music and frequent dis-

cotheques long after those in their age group have ceased to frequent such establishments, reverential church music also makes a strong appeal to them and the organ is their instrument. They respond best to music in E-natural.

Scarlatti's Sonata in E; Bach's Concerto No. 2 in E for violin.

Virgo (23 August–23 September): the sign of the intellectual of precision, clarity and thought. This does not mean that all Virgoans are intellectuals, for in the horoscopes of some other signs may also influence them. These natives are apt to be perfectionists, however, are often pedantic or finicky, and frequently suffer from duodenal ulcers and intestinal troubles caused by their pernickety natures, for unlike Taureans they rarely explode in anger and so rid themselves of repressions. Outwardly they often remain calm and unruffled while inwardly they seethe. They have no particular tonal affinity but respond best to the works of composers like Bach, Honegger, Bartok – even Chopin and John Field – whose compositions have meticulously detailed tonal constructions.

Libra (24 September–23 October): these lovers of grace, rhythm and balance make fine dancers and musicians, for they respond to sheer melody and to music in E-sharp and G-flat. They love 'sweet' music, often of the sugary kind, the sort which creates abstract images or auditory beauty, but sheer away from pieces in which technical construction or form is the composer's main object.

Generally speaking Librans love the music of Johann Strauss and the light operas but they also appreciate music such as Beethoven's Sonata No. 24 in F-sharp major and Rachmaninoff's Concerto No. 1 in F-sharp for piano, Op. 1. -

Scorpio (24 September–22 November): these natives are usually decisive, aggressive, magnetic and robust. They dislike environmental noise but have strong recuperative powers and listening to music in G-natural helps them to overcome stress.

Bach's Partita No. 5 in G; Beethoven's Variations (12) in G.

Sagittarius (23 November–20 December): here one finds the extroverts who love life and show it; the nature and animal lovers who prefer country to town and fly to it at every opportunity; confident, open, impulsive, with a cheerful outlook. They are the athletes, hunters and travellers and prefer the sort of music Souza composed and pieces such as Chopin's Waltz No. 8 in A-flat major, Op. 64, No. 3; Dvorak's Quartet No. 7 in A-flat; Mendelssohn's Concerto in A-flat for two pianos and orchestra, and Elgar's symphony No. 1 in A-flat, for their natures respond best to tunes in G-sharp and A-flat.

Capricorn (21 December–19 January): those born under the sign of the Goat are opposites, as far as music is concerned, to natives of Scorpio. They are hard-working, reliable, ambitious for material things, and eager for worldly recognition. They are the climbers. Abrasive sounds upset their equilibrium and noise makes them irritable and liable to retreat into their shells. Their serious nature makes them lovers of the heavier kinds of classical music, for they have an inner sensitivity which responds to pieces which declaim the good earth and its products.

All music in A-natural: Bach's Concerto No. 4 in A for harpsichord; Beethoven's Symphony No. 7 in A, Op. 92; Mozart's Concerto in A.

Aquarius (20 January–19 February): Sun Aquarians are easy going, tolerant, likeable, witty and creative; interested in causes rather than individuals, who will beggar their families for the benefit of humanity. Their minds are quick and flexible, for they belong to the age of the computer, the jet plane and the intercontinental ballistic missile. The music they respond to best is in A-sharp and B-flat, and they gain mental and spiritual pabulum from pieces such as Brahms' Concerto No. 2 in B-flat for piano, Op. 83; Chopin's Sonata No. 2 in B-flat for piano, Op. 35; or Mozart's Serenade in B-flat or Piano Concerto in B-flat.

Pisces: (20 February–20 March): the sign of the sympathetic, the understanding and the saints. Pisceans are warm-hearted, imbued with strong religious feeling and psychic to a degree. They gravitate towards psychology, the priesthood, the more sober of the arts, and chemistry.

The tired and jaded Piscean is likely to take to 'pot' and tranquillizers but can gain fuller refreshment from music, especially in B-natural; from masses and passions and Gregorian chants and chorals in Latin, which need no understanding, for they live in the spirit.

Brahms's Trio No. 1 in B for violin and cello, Op. No. 8 is ideal, or Haydn's symphony No. 46.

RE-LEARNING

The science of vibrations is in its infancy and we have merely touched the fringe of its possibilities. It may have been known in great detail to the Ancient Hindus, the Chinese and the Mayans, but such knowledge was lost either through their own folly, greed and misuse, or through cataclysms such as earthquakes, tidal waves and volcanic eruptions which wiped out entire civilizations, such as Atlantis and the Minoan kingdom. It seems that every few millenniums civilizations are destroyed and those coming after have painfully to learn what their ancestors knew.

JIVAKA, THE KING OF DOCTORS

As far back as the fifth century BC the *Atharva-Veda** records that in the town of Taxila there was a medical school of high repute and that the Principal, a doctor named Jivaka, performed miracles of surgery by means of a marvellous gem which was used to light up the interior of patients' bodies, as a lamp lights a room. It is now known that Indian surgeons of the period used more than 150 surgical instruments to per-

---

* *Veda* means knowledge. The *Vedas* consist of the *Rig-Veda Yajur-Veda*, *Sama-Veda* and *Atharva-Veda*.

form all sorts of intricate operations. By means of this 'gem'
Jivaka would look into the head of a patient, see a 'centipede'
(brain tumour or cyst), open the skull and remove it. The
instrument used was a 'golden pincers'. Could the gem have
been a form of X-ray and the golden pincers a laser beam?
Who knows?

THE EMPEROR HAO-TSU

The Emperor Hao-tsu, who founded the Han Dynasty about
the year 206 BC, was also a physician of considerable repute,
and one of his discoveries was 'a precious mirror that illumi-
nates the bones of the body'. It is described as

> a rectangular mirror four feet wide, five feet and nine
> inches high, brilliant both on its outer and inner sides.
> When a man stood straight before it to see his reflection his
> image appeared reversed. When someone placed his hands
> on his heart he observed the five viscera placed side by side
> and not impeded by any obstacle.
>
> When a man had a hidden malady within his organs, he
> could recognize the seat of his complaint by looking into the
> mirror and laying his hands on his heart. *

Obviously it was some sort of X-ray machine.

GONDWANA

Who knows what knowledge the people of Gondwana, the
super-continent which united all the southern continents and
Australia in the past, had acquired and accumulated? Professor M. G. Ravich, the Soviet polar scientist, said:

> During my scientific mission to Australia more than a year
> ago I had the chance to visit the surrounds of Adelaide, on

* L. Giles, *A Gallery of Chinese Immortals* (John Murray, 1948).

the Pacific coast, where I had a big geological journey collecting rock samples. The samples were carefully analysed in the laboratories of the Arctic Geology Institute in Leningrad and their absolute age, chemical and other specific features were determined. After that I carried out a comparative study of the Australian samples and the Antarctic rock samples that were collected by geologists of the Soviet Antarctic Expeditions.*

Though thousands of miles apart the character of the rock systems of Australia and Antarctica had much in common, not only in their composition but in their thickness and the way in which they were spread.

Each system was found to date back 2000 million years. Perhaps they were once inhabited, but what became of the people and the knowledge they must have accumulated? The Aborigines seem to be their sole descendants, and they, as scientists are now discovering, have much secret knowledge and a religion many centuries older but similar in many respects to Christianity!

LASERS

Today our understanding of matter and vibrations continues apace. About fifteen years ago Dr Theodore M. Maiman, of the Hughes Aircraft Corporation, California, succeeded in producing a light source hitherto unknown, called Light Amplification by Stimulated Emission of Radiation (LASER), and within days scientists in Britain who had been working on the same lines produced the same results.

Lasers can kill or cure, depending on the way they are used. They can be used as scalpels to perform delicate operations on the retina, to control glaucoma, to excise cancerous growths, and for use in precision engineering. They can also destroy

* Novosti Information Service.

tissue, cut through the toughest steel and be employed as death rays. It is for Man to decide.

MATTER

Our ideas about the nature of matter are also changing. The Soviet physicists Victor Ginzburg and Professor Boris Bolotovsky demonstrated to the USSR Academy of Sciences evidence which tends to overturn the theory that nothing moves faster than light. They organized an experiment which showed the reflection of a beam running along a wall at a speed faster than that of light! This they say is of immense importance in the physics of pulsars, the exact nature of which has not as yet been determined.

We are on the verge of new and exciting discoveries about the way vibrations act, and one hopes that this new knowledge will be used for the development and happiness of mankind and not for its destruction.

Index